PARENTING
from the heart

By Marilyn Boyer

PRACTICAL PAR___
FROM A MOM OF 14 CHILDREN

Parenting from the Heart
© 2004 by Marilyn Boyer
Published 2004, 2009.
Printed in the United States of America.

ISBN 0-9708770-0-5
978-0-9708770-7-9

Cover design by Katie Karman.

Published by The Learning Parent
2430 Sunnymeade Road
Rustburg, VA 24588
www.thelearningparent.com

The Learning Parent is dedicated to equipping and encouraging home school
families to raise their children in the nurture and admonition of the Lord.
*"That the generation to come might know, even the children yet to be born, that they may arise and tell
them to their children, that they should put their confidence in God, and not forget the works of God,
but keep His commandments."*
Psalm 78:6-7

Also by Rick & Marilyn Boyer:

The Hands-on Dad
Rick shares seven Biblical functions for the father and shows how they apply in home education. These important and practical insights can set both Mom and Dad free to be their best for their children. **$9.95**

Home Educating with Confidence
Rick and Marilyn Boyer share their experiences to encourage and equip others. You don't have to be a child psychologist or have a fancy degree to raise godly children. **$9.95**

Fun Projects for Hands-on Character Building
The Boyers share their philosophy of spiritual training with scores of practical, effective, and enjoyable projects. **$9.95**

Yes, They're all Ours
The story of the Boyer family – what life is like with 14 children, and why we chose to live this way. Also includes humorous anecdotes. **$9.95**

Homemade with Love
Marilyn Boyer shares her tried and true recipes for feeding 14 hungry children economically and simply. **$9.95**

The Runt
Rick Boyer shares with young readers the fictional adventures of a boy and his unpromising, mongrel pup. With that scrap of a dog, God teaches what it really means to be a winner. **$9.95**

Bible Curriculum
Character Qualities flashcards
Cards feature a question and picture to color on the front, and a verse on the back. For example: "Why should we choose godly friends?" Answer: "He who walks with wise men shall be wise.

But the companion of fools suffers harm." Proverbs 13:20 **$5.00**

If/When flashcards
Teach your children what to do in certain situations. For example: "When tempted to hate correction" (Proverbs 12:1)? Answer: "Whoever loves discipline loves knowledge, but he who hates reproof is stupid." **$5.00**

Proverbs flashcards
Teach your children Bible verses from the Book of Wisdom. Each card features a picture for your child to color. **$5.00**

Proverbs for Preschoolers
Children learn the principles in Proverbs while practicing stylus skills, memorizing the alphabet, and coloring. **$12.95**

Proverbs People I & II
Workbooks that use short-answer questions, stories, quizzes, and coloring pages to teach character qualities to children 8 to 12. **Vol I: $11.95 Vol II: $10.95**

Living the Fruitful Life
A Bible study course on how to apply the fruit of the Spirit to our lives. For middle-school students. **$12.95**

Power in Proverbs
A self-led concordance study guide for teenagers. **$10.95**

To request a free catalog of the previous books as well as a whole range of Christian home school materials, please contact The Learning Parent at:
(434) 845-8345
2430 Sunnymeade Road
Rustburg, VA 24588
www.TheLearningParent.com

Table of Contents

Introduction

     This book is the result of the passion of my heart for you and your family. I want to see you reach your full potential of effectiveness for God. I'm burdened by the condition of families in our country as a whole, but I'm excited for our future because of moms and dads just like you who are dedicated to doing whatever it takes to train children to be mighty warriors for our Lord Jesus.

     God wants us to be the salt and light in this current generation and He has an exciting plan for your family to be involved. Anyone can be a successful parent. The only ingredient required is a heart wholly devoted to Jesus Christ in whom we place our trust for eternal salvation.

     God has graciously blessed me with fourteen children; eight girls and six boys. Motherhood has been a way of life for me now for almost thirty years. Training little ones to serve their Maker is what it's all about. I wouldn't trade having fourteen kids for any other life style. It's been an honor to raise them to love and serve their Savior, and it is to my kids and my wonderful husband that I dedicate this book.

     It is in serving all of you and my Savior that I have found deep fulfillment in my own life, and the thing that blesses me most is observing how each one of you desire to be used by God in His mighty plan for eternity.

     May each one of you pass on the torch of faithfulness to your children, and to God be the glory for all eternity!

 Chapter 1

So now you're a mommy!

I suppose every new mom feels it – the joy of holding this new little life, and at the same time the awesome responsibility of knowing this little person is entirely dependent on her! I think of all the times I've sought advice from more experienced parents, wished there was a magic formula for rearing Godly children. Now, after 30 years and 14 children, I've learned there is no magic formula.

And now I often end up on the receiving end of those "young mom" questions. I watch parents struggle for answers, seeking God's best for their families. I would love to have all the answers. I don't, but He does. And He is still teaching me every day.

As I reflect back on all the lessons, as I try to answer questions the best I can, I often wish I could do more to help so many searching young moms. If I had one desire, it would be to share what God has taught me, and perhaps see it help one more mom.

That's how this book came about. It's not really a parenting manual, but more of a mom-to-mom talk, my own parenting story. If God can use any of the principles He has taught me, if something I've learned can encourage you in your parenting journey, I'd love nothing more.

So come on over, prop your feet up, grab a cup of coffee, and let's talk!

Growing up, I was the youngest of three girls. My sister and I spent hours playing dolls and pretending we were mommies. As I got older, I had lots of babysitting jobs. I loved kids! When I was dating Rick, I made it clear to him that I loved children and wanted 'several'. Rick was in the Air Force when we got married, and we got stationed in Florida shortly after our marriage. I guess you could say we married young. I was eighteen, Rick was twenty.

I couldn't wait to be a mommy!

For me, that wonderful event occurred on my 20th birthday! Little Rickey entered the world, weighing in at 8 lb., 14 oz. He began squalling just after he was born and has been going headstrong ever since. He was a man with a mission, even as an infant.

Even though I was hardly more than a child myself and being in a strange place away from home, as I held my newborn little son, I was ready to tackle the job. This pride and joy I felt sunk in, as did the realization that he was totally dependent upon me.

Let me interject here some thoughts on childbirth. I decided I wanted as much as possible to trust God's plan and schedule and timing, so my aim with all my pregnancies was to let God bring about labor and delivery in His way, which for me meant the least amount of intrusion medically. I often had to beg my doctor to wait and let labor happen instead of inducing. If you can just wait and let it happen naturally you'll find that God does so much preparatory work. I didn't use any drugs during delivery, after Rickey's delivery, that is.

I think often the medical establishment plays on the anticipation and weariness of the mom who just wants it over with, and unnecessary problems are created. If you can, just let God do it. He created us and He knows best, and doing it naturally is definitely better for both mom and baby with a much faster recovery time.

Sometimes problems do occur and God is in control of them too, but just don't help to cause trouble by impatience. We had four home births along the way, but then found some great doctors who let us do it our way and let me go home about six to ten hours after delivery.

That doesn't mean labor and delivery were easy for me; quite the contrary. Two of my labors were short. The rest were very long, stopping and starting for what seemed like days. I would almost lie awake nights and remember previous deliveries and think, "God, I can't do this again," but I always seemed to manage, depending on God. I would ask God for a special verse, and he gave me one for each labor. I would memorize it beforehand and constantly quote it throughout all of delivery.

I never did all the breathing stuff, although I did take learning classes with my second baby. I found them very helpful in recognizing what the stages of labor were so I could cooperate with what God was trying to accomplish in each stage. It helped me to understand, but scripture, not breathing, is what held me together.

Now that he was born, what next? I read all the

books on child rearing, although there were not a lot back then - what there was were mostly academic so I gleaned what I could from them. I never found a fast-and-hard philosophy that I could adopt as my own, so I had to rely on God to impress on my heart how He wanted me to rear my children, and He did just that.

Our children are gifts from God, entrusted to us for a brief amount of time, ordained by God. Our utmost mission is to train them to love and serve their Savior. Therefore, my philosophy for child rearing developed from being sensitive to God's Spirit in my life as well as gleaning insights from scripture.

I proceeded to study God's word to find how God deals with us, His children. As I read the Bible in this light, God confirmed through scripture the impressions that He had laid on my heart:

A newborn baby is born into the world totally dependent on us as parents. He/she is born with all the potential in the world to accomplish great and mighty feats for God. Our job is but to point and steer and lead in the right direction.

Crying, as opposed to what some people believe, is not bad. It is a newborn's only way of communication with his parents to let them know he has a need. God deals with us in much the same way, and it is so encouraging to remember as a new parent that God doesn't expect us to have all the answers. His plan is for us to sense our need and cry out to Him for wisdom. He, in truth, is just waiting to pour out His wisdom and guidance on us. He does want us to cry out (Pr. 8) and to realize our dependence on Him.

We can't make it on our own.

When our newborn baby cries out for us, that's our cue to find and meet his need. Maybe it's time for a feeding, a diaper change, or maybe he just needs the security of knowing we are there. That's when it's time to sit and rock them and tell them how special they are, that they are created in God's image, and how much we love them and enjoy holding them, singing to them, etc. Don't buy into that ridiculous theory of waiting until a baby stops crying before you pick it up!

I held my babies a lot! I didn't think I could ever tire of snuggling a newborn. Newborn days pass so quickly. I didn't want to miss a minute of it. It's time that you never get back.

Call it bonding if you like, but babies need time with Mom and Dad. They need to gain security from the sound of your voice, the touch of your hands ("Then I was by Him, as one brought up with Him, and I was daily His delight, rejoicing always before Him" Prov. 8:30) just as we need time with God; time enough to sense His Spirit's promptings in our soul, time to feel the purifying water of the Word in our lives and the comforting presence of His Spirit. Why does God call us His children? Could it be that He wants to show us a picture of how we need to treat our children? Babies need to be touched and snuggled and rocked.

I found that each one of my babies was different. Some needed lots of sleep; some needed to nurse every two hours, some every four to five hours. Smaller babies often need to nurse more frequently, as their stomachs can't hold as much.

There are no specific formulas to follow, but I have found that after about 4-6 weeks, each baby would settle into his/her own schedule - the one right for him - and then I could have a pretty good idea of what to expect.

Starting out, I wanted to swing right back into life as soon as possible and just bring my baby along, but with subsequent newborns, I relaxed a little more and just basked in just enjoying this fleeting stage. Like I said, you can't go back in time, so savor this season. Housework will keep, but your baby is growing up fast. My plan was to "maintain" the house – keep clutter picked up, dishes done, etc., but deep cleaning waited.

My babies were almost all two to three weeks late in arriving, so a good plan for me was to do some extra cleaning toward the end of pregnancy, things I knew would bug me afterwards, so I could let things slide a little after the baby was born. I came to the conclusion that for four to six months afterwards, I felt pretty good if I could accomplish one thing each day, besides just maintenance.

God does give times for certain things. Schedules are important. A schedule builds security in a child, but don't go too far and try to set up some idealistic routine that everyone will fit into. Be sensitive to your baby and his needs. Once a pattern emerges, you can plan around that. Make sure you plan for plenty of rocking time, though.

I nursed all my babies, and there is so much evidence now that God's way is best. Breast milk provides baby with natural antibodies and gives him a jump start in life. You've carried him for nine months and felt all his little kicks and hiccups and gotten to know him so much even before he's born, and then the nursing is a precious time and such a security for baby. If you can't nurse for some reason, always hold your baby when you feed him and use it for snuggle time.

I learned to love the nighttime nursing, and that's the feeding my babies usually gave up last (see appendix #1– Teaching Home article). I nursed most of my babies for 15-18 months, longer when I wasn't expecting another right away.

I experimented with making my own baby food and using the store bought kind, but usually I'd just wait until the child began developing an interest for food, reaching out for it, and took that as God's plan for that child. I would feed them mashed potatoes, blended fruit, baby cereals, and as soon as they had some teeth, begin cutting up grapes and strawberries in tiny pieces for them to eat.

My babies seemed to do better waiting until six to ten months and then eating real food in small portions. I never pushed them to drink from a cup, but waited until they were able to handle a sippy cup well. Until then, if I was away, I'd leave juice in a bottle for them. It seems like with the first baby, you tend to be in a hurry to enter all the new stages, but with subsequent babies, you try to slow them down.

Babyhood is fleeting. Enjoy it to the fullest, and don't wish it away. Soon you'll be wishing it back!

My oldest daughter copied this little poem in calligraphy for me years ago and I hung it in my kitchen as a reminder to myself:

"Cleaning and scrubbing can wait 'til tomorrow

So now you're a mommy!

But babies grow up, we've learned to our sorrow.
So quiet down cobwebs, dust, go to sleep,
For I'm rocking my baby, and babies don't keep."

 Chapter Two

Gotta Love Those Toddlers

Just when you're getting things under control a bit, guess what? Here comes baby number two! In our family there were eighteen months between Rickey and Timmy's births, and eighteen to twenty four months between the other babies was pretty much a pattern.

It was very important to me that my first child didn't feel neglected when baby number two came along. As each new one arrived, I began to use nursing time as a special time for the one just older than him. Often when it was time to nurse the newborn, I would call the next child to come sit by me on the couch, and we would read stories.

I never had a big jealousy problem with my kids. Instead of feeling like they were being displaced, the toddler would feel special and look forward to that time. Also, I developed a silly little voice and would pretend that I was the newborn "talking" to the toddler. For instance, when Kelley was born, I would pretend to be her telling Tucker how much I loved him and was so glad he was my big brother. I would tell Tuck, "Quick, tell Snap [his nickname for her] before she forgets," and he would respond with, "I love you SO much, Snap." Kelley would 'tell' Tuck how glad she was to have a big brother to protect her. It may sound silly but really, verbalizing helps little ones to internalize.

Another tip is to let your toddler do things to help with the baby, such as getting diapers and toys. Sometimes I would buy my toddler girls a baby doll so they could diaper and feed their baby while Mommy changed their brother or sister. We also emphasized to the toddlers that the new baby was their brother/sister and they would help Mommy and Daddy care for him/her.

Learn not to resent nighttime nursing. For me, it was a sweet time to spend with my little one. No phone calls, no one calling mommy, no laundry, no knocks on the door, just quietness and my little baby. It's a fleeting season.

Children were not given for our convenience. I've found that my attitude is the key. If I realize that I'm entrusted to rear this little one for our Almighty Creator, then I'm not wasting one minute of my "potential" while I'm changing all those diapers, cleaning up the messes, folding laundry, etc. A verse I always gave my kids to learn was Proverbs 15:1: "A gentle spirit brings life and health, but griping brings discouragement." I would always tell them that it would not only bring discouragement to them but also to others around them. Rest in the fact that God gave you this child and it's His perfect will for you to care for it and do all things as unto the Lord.

As you lose your life in your little one in this "season", it will reap benefits for all of eternity. So, go change another diaper and put in another load of laundry, and do it with a song on your tongue and a deep love in your heart for your little one and for his Creator.

I had always heard, "Watch out for those terrible two's". I really don't think it has anything to do with being two – sometimes it's being three. But it doesn't have to be terrible. It's just another "season" and as always, each toddler handles it differently according to their God-given personality and how you handle it. Some children are very sensitive and respond to "no" by crying. Others are headstrong and test the limits. You and your husband need to get your heads together (over a steak dinner, of course) and set a *few* but *simple* rules of behavior.

Don't expect your child to automatically know what you expect. I remember Carrie, at about a year old, couldn't talk very well yet, and would want to communicate with me, but couldn't get her point across, so she would scream. This "season" didn't last terribly long, but I tried to put myself in her shoes. She was number eight in the lineup, it was hard to get a word in edgewise, and she had trouble mustering up the words anyway. I would try to ask her what the problem was and remedy the situation, but it wasn't always easy. Neither would it have been right to just spank her and expect quietness. She had a frustration and couldn't express it so she had to be taught how to properly express it. It was just a blip in her training - she is now 17 years old and perfectly well adjusted.

The main thing to remember is to deal with your children reasonably and with understanding, as you would want God to deal with you.

16

Then there's Laura, a little bundle of energy (my only child who loved the wind in her face as an infant). She was constantly on the go and making noise. She threw herself into life and made the most of it – loudly. (Her brother coined a special nickname for her: "Mouthy"). I have memories of her as a 15-month old, as I was trying to do school with the others, sitting in the middle of the kitchen table delightedly taking caps off markers and flinging them wildly in every direction. She didn't need a spanking, just loving re-direction.

Life with a toddler doesn't always flow smoothly, but neither does it need to be a constant battle of wills. Stop, pray, ask God for wisdom, try to put yourself in your child's shoes, and *then* correct them. Realize that firmness doesn't mean meanness. The creativity of God is available for the asking.

As a parent, don't let your emotions go unbridled. Go to God first, get your emotions right, and then correct your child. Learn to distinguish childishness from disobedience. There is a difference. Don't expect your toddler to act like an adult. Remember not to react as a toddler might, but ask God to guide your correction.

Potty training doesn't have to be and shouldn't be a big deal. There comes a time in each toddler's life when they're ready, really ready, and if you can be patient and let it occur naturally, it won't be a big deal. Society tends to put pressure on us to have our kids potty trained, and young moms will get together and compare notes on what age little Tommy and Susie were potty trained.

My kids were late, compared to others, and each one

was different from the next, but somewhere between two and four years old they were potty trained. I've found usually when children are trained early, it's more mom being trained to run them to the potty every fifteen minutes than anything else. I didn't have time or interest for that. Training my kids in God's Word was a priority, not using the potty.

When interest came up, I'd show them how, and sometimes give small rewards for using the potty, but I never pressured them or shamed them when they had an accident. When they're a little older, they can wait longer periods of time, and you won't have the problem of having to stop at every public toilet in town. When they're staying dry all night and interested in trying, then begin training, but if you find they're just not catching on, big deal. It's easier to change diapers than having accidents to clean up all over the house and car.

I never had much of a problem with bed wetters by waiting until they were a little older. Often, when a child feels pressure to use the potty and shame or disappointment at accidents, they'll get over-cautious about it and focus on it too much and be afraid of failing. Let them be free to learn in God's timing.

Just relax. If they have trouble with wetting the bed, use diapers just at night – it's usually the deep sleepers that can't wake up soon enough, but it will come. It's no big deal. Don't make them think it is.

At one point, I had three kids in diapers for a few months, but they all learn, and it's just not important what age they are when physically and mentally it clicks and underpants can be bought. That's often an incentive in itself. Also, younger kids will often want to wear big boy pants like big brother does!

Actually, the toddler stage is quite delightful. We get so many laughs and so many of our funny family stories from the toddler years. As you try to guide your toddler in right behavior, think how we must appear to God at times and learn from it. Hold those toddlers a lot. Learn what delights them and be a part of it. Take time to hold that toad, pick a flower, do a leaf rubbing, take a walk in the woods. Toddlers are delighted by their world. Capitalize on their interests and teach them truths about God. Start teaching them scripture. Read to them *a lot*. I remember reading one child's book over eighteen times in one sitting to my firstborn. Say no to lesser things and spend *time* with your toddler. Let him know you delight in him and love being with him.

It has been said that much of a child's character is formed by the time he reaches five years of age. Moses' mother, during the time until she weaned him (about four or five years) had managed to build in him a love for God and sense of destiny for his life.

The toddler years are building-block years of training and teaching. Don't let your time be squandered away.

 Chapter Three

Building A Sense of Destiny In Your Child

"God Made You In A Special Way For A Special Purpose!"

These are words we told our toddlers again and again. It is true! Your child has just as important a role in God's plan for eternity as did Abraham, Moses, Ruth, David. God planned from eternity past for your child (complete with his exact personality) to be born to you and your husband, on the very same day he/she was born, in this time in history, to fulfill a high and holy purpose.

When we get to heaven it's going to be so neat to see how things that Abraham, Isaac, and Jacob did that affected others also affected us, and how things that we do and decisions we make and accomplishments we achieve will affect others yet to be born. Heaven will be an eternity full of "flipping the tapestry" – things that looked like a tangled mess down here will be revealed as part of God's exciting plan for the ages up there, and your child is part of that plan. Our job is to convey this truth to our children and help them discover God's exciting plans for their lives.

We've made each one of our children a "Jesus plaque" that we hang by their bed. Each night before going to sleep, the last thing they see is a visual representation that Jesus personally loves and cares about them. We pray and thank God that He has a special plan for Kelley and Kasey's life and that no one in all the world can do what God has in store for them to do. We sing this little song that a dear friend of ours, Jana Getz, wrote to the tune of Jesus Loves Me:

"I am special, this I know,
For the Bible tells me so.
God knew me before my birth
And planned each day of my life on earth.

"I am fashioned by God's hand
Unto good works throughout the land
For in Him I'll learn to be
All He's prepared especially for me.

"Even though I make mistakes
God forgives for His Name's sake.
He helps me to be kind and good
And helps me do the things I should.

"I am precious in God's sight
And in Him my soul delights

He loves me and died for me
That I might live eternally."

Personalize your prayers as you pray with your child – insert their name as you pray. Encourage your child to pray throughout the day. Let them know that God's power is always available to them. They can call on God anytime, anywhere, and He's always there. Even if you're not around, they can cry out to God for help and He hears them and cares about them. Thank God that "Kelley was nice to Kasey today" (and watch the corners of their mouths turn up in a smile) as you speak their name in prayer to God.

Teach your child the meaning of their name. We do many things to remind our child of the meaning of their name. We make a name plaque for each child, including a Bible verse, to hang in their bedroom. In our book "Fun Projects for Hands-On Character Building", we have a whole section of projects for teaching kids the meaning of their name. "The Name Book" is an excellent resource for finding the literal and spiritual meanings of names and it suggests a Bible verse for each.

We always carefully chose our children's names before they were born, and we've been amazed at how they tend to live up to the meaning of their name. Our Emily (meaning "diligent") is now nineteen years old. She has started a business cleaning houses and even at home is constantly picking up messes, putting things in order, etc. Her room is always neat. Rick, our oldest (meaning "brave, strong ruler"), has from a little boy desired to be a statesman and a godly politician. God planted that desire in his little heart and cultivated it, and at the age of nineteen, Rick ran for chairman of our county Republican party and won. Just last year he ran for Supervisor, an elected official in his county, and unseated an incumbent truant officer. God instilled in him a bold and fearless spirit and a great desire for truth and righteousness to prevail, without compromise.

And so it goes, God has a plan and it is always ultimately good and right. So, tonight as you tuck your little ones into bed, pray with vision, and open for them, as it were, the skies of heaven and give them a peek!

 Chapter Four

Building A Heart Of Obedience

What is our goal concerning obedience? It's not to have our children do whatever pleases us, but whatever pleases our Savior. Remember that when their behavior is bugging you and you're tempted to snap at them to stop whatever they're doing "because I said so", and remember how God deals with us as children - firmly, not harshly, with love, and for our good.

We are all sinners, I know, but I still believe that most children start out wanting to please their parents and desire to attain their parents' approval. We just need to make our instructions clear and therefore easier to obey. They won't always obey, but don't exasperate them and make it harder.

I would describe my child training philosophy as a proactive, discipleship relationship - parenting from the heart, touching the child's heart.

Let me tell you of an experience we had and how it

shaped how we trained our children. I was grocery shopping one day; I think I had five children at the time, all 7 years old and under. They weren't being bad, they were just THERE. Everywhere. I was bumping the cart into them, they were asking for all the goodies on the shelves, you get the picture. At home that evening I was trying to explain my frustration to Rick when he came up with a great idea that had significant impact on our child training experience.

He suggested that we go to the grocery store that evening with the express purpose of training the kids how to behave. I walked along, picking up a few items and he walked beside me, giving the kids just a few simple rules – walk behind Mom and the cart, don't touch anything on the shelves, make your requests for food at home before we go to the store, etc. The result was incredible. The very next time I took them shopping, I began getting comments from fellow shoppers: "How do you get your children to be so well behaved?"

We were encouraged, the kids were encouraged when people noticed their behavior, and we decided to try training them for other situations too. At the time I was pregnant, and not having any children old enough to babysit or my parents close by or money to spare, I would have to take all the children with me when I went for my doctor visits. With five different personalities and my oldest being only 7, you can imagine that it wasn't easy.

I prepared them as best I could for what to expect, how long Mom would be, and prepared a bag of activities to take with us. Rickey, being the oldest, was in charge while Mom was back seeing the doctor. He was given the job of reading to others, distributing puzzles, coloring books and crayons with Tim's help, and basically being responsible to see that they followed instructions. He did and they did, and to this day, the people in the office talk of how obedient our children were. On the way home, as promised, we stopped at a little market for a treat – cheese popcorn. My kids still remember it as the "cheese popcorn store".

We also applied the principle to other situations: going to restaurants, a friend's house, etc., and explaining what to expect and how we expected them to act. We would make it into a game, practicing on the way to the restaurant. "When the waitress gives you a glass of water, what do you say?" "Thank you".

Like I said, they won't always obey, and I'll discuss in a moment how we handle disobedience, but it is true that if you're positive, prepare in advance, and praise them for good behavior, you're on the right track.

We drilled into our children the fact that others were watching them (and in our family, nothing could be more true). We had a large crew and people did notice! Often the kids would say, "Mom, they're counting us again." Sure enough, there was a lady, pointing, counting, and exclaiming, "...four, five, six, SEVEN KIDS!"

We told our children that they represented Jesus to people around them and they would either be a help or a hindrance in bringing others to the Lord by their behavior. They would influence others either positively or negatively for God's kingdom and for home education and the testimony of a large family in today's society. We told them often that God wants us all to shine as lights in the midst of a crooked and evil generation (Phil. 2:15).

We had a special experience that encouraged us all and confirmed to our children that what we said was true. One day we took our six kids to Golden Corral for supper (a treat in those days). We noted a man casting many glances in our direction as we were eating our supper. He finally came over to our table and told us he was a pastor from a neighboring town and how impressed he was with the behavior of our children. We thanked him and he went back to his seat, and we resumed eating our meal. When we finished and Rick went up to pay, he was waiting in line with the check, when the gentleman came up behind him and took the bill and told Rick that he was touched and blessed by the example of so many children being obedient for such an extended time, that he paid for our meal! Boy, was that ever sweet! Funds were never easy to come by and it was such a confirmation and blessing both to us and our kids that something simple like just obeying affects those around us. People take notice when they see obedient, respectful children.

Okay, I know what you're thinking – "so what happens when they don't obey?" And yes, I have had the other kind of experiences, too. I remember so clearly the day I took Christa, Laura, Brittany and Tucker to K-Mart. By this time, I had older children for babysitters and usually I left the younger ones at home to play instead of dragging them around to do countless errands, like I had to when my oldest children were young.

Well, Laura needs a word of explanation. She was born loud. She has a great zest for life and is not shy about expressing it. She was loud without even realizing it. When something upset her, you knew about it! Anyway, I was busy crossing things off my list; Christa (quiet instigator type) meanwhile, did something to irritate Laura, and Laura, in a fit of irritation, threw the hand mirror I was planning to purchase on the floor, shattering it into a million pieces, and then began crying when she saw what happened. Yes, I wanted to fall through the floor and disappear. It was then that I realized, hey, I did a good job training my older kids how to act in stores, but now I've got to do it all over again. These younger ones are missing a crucial part of their education! By the way, Laura is now fourteen years old, a delightful young lady who enjoys people and loves life, and doesn't throw mirrors anymore.

So, what happens when they disobey? First of all, we teach our children that obedience has three aspects to it: It must be done cheerfully, immediately, and thoroughly. If any one of these aspects is missing, it is not obedience. A grudging, griping spirit, dragging your feet and procrastination, or not doing a thorough job just doesn't constitute true obedience.

We correct our kids for three things: Disobedience (direct defiance to a specific command), disrespect, and irresponsibility.

Be careful to distinguish disobedience from childishness. Spilling milk is childishness in most cases. Remember that your child is a child. Don't expect them to act as if they had the maturity of an adult. And remember that you spill milk sometimes too!

Here are a few simple guidelines we follow:

1. We will instruct our child what we want them to do. If your child is young - a toddler or preschooler - have them repeat the instruction back to you. Get on your knees or pull them onto your lap and look in their eyes instead of just shouting out a command.

2. Warn. If they disobey, give them the benefit of the doubt and repeat your instruction. "Remember, what did Mommy tell you to do?" Have them repeat it back. Let them know if they do it again you'll have to handle it as disobedience. We explain to our kids that God has an umbrella of protection over us. When we obey Mom or Dad, we're learning to obey God, and his umbrella of protection covers us and keeps us safe.

3. Correction. If your child persists in the behavior, you will have to correct him/her. Always use scripture to establish wrongdoing. Example: Kari says unkind words to John. John gets angry and pulls Kari's hair. Ephesians 4:26, "Be angry, and sin not. Let not the sun go down upon wrath." Use the best method of correction for the child. When you spank, use a neutral object which can't damage the child. For some children, other correction works as well or better. For example, if my oldest son needed correction while company was over, the worst thing you could do was send him to his room by himself. He loved to be in the center of things. Also, we sometimes withdraw privileges. Be firm, but not harsh.

4. Show love. Affirm to your child that you love him and are only following God's plan for instituting discipline in his life, not trying to be mean. If the child has offended someone, they must ask forgiveness or even make

restitution. If they break someone's toy, for instance, have them do jobs to earn money to pay for a new one. In the event of anger, instruct them as to God's way to handle the situation. Proverbs 15:1: "A soft answer turns away wrath, but grievous words stir up anger." Next time, instead of giving in to anger, prepare a gentle answer and stand back and watch God work.

Now, just a couple of training tips. We had a friend who had a son, David. One day David walked between two parked cars and was about to head into the street into the path of an oncoming vehicle. David was too short to see the car. His dad saw the danger and called out, "David, STOP!" David did stop, and his life was spared. We used that true story to illustrate to our children that parents often foresee dangers that lie ahead, dangers that our children are unaware of. Our children must learn to instantly obey their parents. We tell our kids that we'll be glad to explain later, but they must obey first and then ask why.

To help instill this in our kids, Rick made up a fun game. We called it obedience exercises. (I know the neighbors must have thought we were crazy for this one). We'd take the kids out in the yard and have them line up at one end of the yard. Rick would holler out commands such as, "Sit!" "Run!" "Stop!" "Lie down!" "Walk backwards!" "Run!" "Walk like a crab!", etc., and the kids would follow the command as quickly as possible. It was hilarious to watch, especially as the toddlers tried to join in also, usually one or two commands behind the rest. Everyone laughed and had a good time, and as a consequence, got into the habit of obeying first-time commands. It was enjoyed by everyone and often the kids would beg to do obedience exercises when company would come over and we had "double the kids."

One other game we played to teach wise choices was a game we called "Ifs". We would think of situations we knew our kids would face in day to day life in interaction with others, and quiz them on what decision they ought to make. For example, we'd say, "Rick, what if you were at Travis' house and he said, 'Come on Rick, let's watch TV. This is a good program. Your mom wouldn't mind,' what would you do?" "Tim, suppose you were at church and Jeremy said, 'Tim, let's go throw berries at the girls,' what would you do?"

Just to let you know if it had any effect, see in the appendix a quote from my oldest son, Rick (Appendix 3).

What we found, in a nutshell, is that if you'll invest time in training beforehand, keeping a few simple, easy-to-understand rules, and encourage right behavior, that disciplinary measures won't be needed nearly as often. As a matter of fact, we found that we didn't need to give out nearly as many spankings with our little ones as we did with the older ones, because they grow up seeing obedience as a normal pattern, and seeing disobedience resulting in unpleasant consequences. Each child is different - temperaments vary, some are compliant, some strong willed, but these principles are general guidelines and can benefit anyone.

So gather the kids and have a good laugh on the front lawn!

 Chapter Five

Saturate Your Home With Scripture

What is saturation? If you add sugar to water bit by bit, you finally get to saturation point when no more sugar will dissolve in the water. The water is then thoroughly sweet. So it is with scripture. We hear the Word, hear some more, hear some more, and finally become so familiar with it that it becomes a part of us and our behavior is changed. "For My thoughts are not your thoughts, saith the Lord, neither are your ways my ways, saith the Lord. For as the heavens are higher than the earth, so are my ways higher than your ways and my thoughts than your thoughts" (Isaiah 55: 8-9). Our goal is to actually exchange our thoughts for God's thoughts, and when God's Word is alive in our everyday lives, guiding the choices we make and the thoughts we think, we become more and more like Jesus.

That's our goal for ourselves and our kids. By the way mom, as you spend time teaching your kids God's Word, explaining it to them, you in fact are meditating on it, and it becomes part of you; you're not just teaching your children what they need to know to become successful adults, you're becoming a successful adult yourself.

As we pour ourselves into meeting the needs of our children (losing our own lives, as it were), we find we are well on the way to having a successful, productive life ourselves. ("For whosoever will save his life shall lose it; and whosoever will lose his life for my sake shall find it" Matt. 16:25). Isn't God's plan wonderful?

When Rickey, my oldest child, was born, I was all charged up to raise a super-kid. I'd always wanted to be a teacher. I went to college for one year, got two years' credit, and had only one teaching course before getting married at the age of eighteen. I was moving away from home (Rick was in the Air Force at the time), and fifteen months later, having my first child. So I was pumped to make him a super kid. We lived in a trailer at the time, as Rick was attending college, and I had the walls plastered with ABC's. Rickey had learned them by the time he was eighteen months, and he could point to all the ABC's and make a pretty decent attempt at saying them all.

About this time, we started attending a Sunday school class for which I will eternally be grateful. It was taught by a man named Larry Coy, who encouraged us to learn how to internalize God's Word in our hearts to change our everyday lives. Rick and I were like sponges. Sunday school never lasted long enough for us. We'd get writer's cramp every week taking notes, and all during the week I would ask God to show me a way to communicate these awesome principles of life to my little Rickey.

We were broke, but becoming richer every day as we saw God's Word penetrate our hearts and lives and lead us in the paths of righteousness. The ABC's came off the walls and Bible verses went up, and Rick and I began committing passages of scripture to memory. James 1 was the first chapter, and if you had walked into our humble living room, you'd have seen it, big as life, written in marker on old construction paper and taped to our paneled walls; but we learned it.

I began making Bible verses on 5x7 cards for Rickey, illustrating them with stick figures (I never was artistically inclined), but Rickey didn't care. As a matter of fact, he began learning massive amounts of scripture for a 2-year-old. It was easy for him. He loved it and we loved it and cheered him on. Rick and I, both having been saved at the age of sixteen, saw huge changes in our own lives and our little boy was becoming mighty in spirit. God's Word is the ONLY thing that permanently changes and molds our lives.

Our family grew. We bought our first house and moved out in the country. I didn't have much company, so I gave myself to teaching my boys scripture. I'd ask God for ideas and He delighted in dropping ideas into my head – ways to make scripture a part of their surroundings.

I made each boy a Character Sketch quilt, using Bill Gothard's Character Sketch books (see www.iblp.org). They are big thick books that give stories about animals in nature that demonstrate particular character qualities, and stories of people in scripture who demonstrated that same quality. Kids relate so well to animals. I remember my little 3-year-old Timmy happily proclaiming, "Mommy, I was orderly just like the woodchuck!" On the front of the quilt blocks were a picture of the animal, the character quality it demonstrates, and a definition of the quality. On the back side of the quilt was a Bible verse to learn. We used these quilts every naptime to teach scripture. The kids would choose which animal to do each day. (Instructions for this quilt are detailed in "Fun Projects for Hands-On Character Building").

The kids' bedroom, in fact, was saturated with scripture. Covering the windows were curtains, colored by the kids using fabric crayons, showing Bible characters and qualities they demonstrated in their lives. Hanging by each child's bed was a picture of Jesus holding their face in his hands, helping them to visualize that Jesus personally loves them.

Also adorning the walls were name plaques reminding the child of the meaning of their name. We carefully chose their names. "The Name Book" is an excellent resource to help with scriptural meanings of names. The older boys for a long while shared a room with the Noah's Ark theme. I made macramé animals to hang on the walls, and each had a Bible name, ex.: Jeremiah the Giraffe, Enoch the Elephant, etc. Across the top of the walls was a chart, the ABC Bible men chart. A – Abraham, FAITH- And God counted it to him as righteousness (Romans 4:20-22). (For full A-Z project see appendix 4). Each letter was represented by a Bible character, had an outstanding quality for that person, and a Bible verse to learn. I let the boys make plaques for the walls with church bulletins containing pictures and verses.

Another project was the "Rickey Board". The first one was made out of scrap plywood we found at the dump.

I had Rickey lie down, traced his outline on the wood and Rick cut it out with his jigsaw. Around the edges we placed Bible verses I'd looked up in the concordance that showed him how to use his head down to his feet for Jesus (Instructions in "Fun Projects for Hands-On Character Building"). It was based on Romans 12:1-2, encouraging Rickey to give his body as a living sacrifice for his Lord. In later years, we updated it and took a picture of Gracie, enlarged it to poster size, cut it out and attached it to backing, wrote verses around it, and put it in a poster frame (size 28x30).

We found that our kids were interested in helping us make the projects and the fact that the projects were personalized motivated them all the more to learn those scriptures.

Each room in the house had a theme. The kitchen was God's provision. Rick and I had a quilt on our bed with the responsibilities of husband and wife to each other and I Corinthians 13 on it. The living room was God's promises. My goal was to get scripture before our eyes to make a difference in our lives. By the way, I'm not even creative. God is though, and all the ideas I just told you about are simple to do. If you have older children, encourage them to help do projects with the little ones. God's Word is alive, it's precious, and it changes lives. Make it a priority!

 Chapter Six

Character Counts

Character does count. Our Founding Fathers certainly thought so. It's been said, "Character is doing what's right when nobody's looking." This is what we must instill in our children. Scripture is loaded with positive and negative examples of character. Character is basically the attributes of God. Our goal is to be like Jesus, and therefore we want to teach our children what character qualities mean so they can adopt them into their lives.

Character Sketches, as I mentioned in the last chapter, has been a mainstay in our home, as have "A Child's Book Of Character Building", vols.1 and 2. These books give simple definitions that kids can understand, for example: "Attentiveness = listening with ears, eyes and heart", and then apply it to daily situations as well as giving a Bible character who exemplified the quality.

Consider personalizing the character qualities for your children to make it easier for them to apply. For example, see appendix #2 to see character qualities I've personalized for myself. It's so effective to personalize scripture and character qualities to bring about real changes in our lives.

Remember that a negative character trait in our lives is just a positive character quality misused. God will often take our biggest weaknesses and make them our biggest strengths. So don't despair when you see character deficiencies in yourself or your children. God's at work. Get busy teaching your kids what character is and God will use that to do the changing.

Gear scriptures to be learned to specific character needs you see in your child. For instance, if unkindness is a problem, use your concordance and find references to kindness, and assign those verses to your child to learn, or make them into 3x5 cards for your little ones.

We never put our children into AWANA, although our church does have that program. The reason is that we knew our kids would do well. We started early teaching them scripture. But scripture is for the purpose of changing our behavior, and we geared memory work to character needs in order to see scripture change lives. I felt it would instead promote a spirit of competition and pride in my kids if they'd been in AWANA. I didn't want to create a stumbling block for them in focusing on winning a prize. AWANA is great for kids who aren't getting scripture at home. Sunday schools were created to be an outreach and that's fine, but it wasn't the best choice for our children.

God holds parents responsible to train and guide and steer their children in His paths. We have rewarded our children for learning scripture, such as a new tropical fish for learning ten verses, or a book they want, etc. But it's a goal that's achievable for them, not competing even with brothers or sisters in achieving it.

If I could emphasize one thing in the training of your children, perhaps the best thing we've done, it would be Bible tapes. When our oldest kids were young, Rick began making sets of Bible tapes. He would read through Proverbs, then Psalms, Matthew, etc., stopping occasionally to explain difficult words and giving stories to illustrate different concepts. He's a good storyteller. We would then play tapes at naptime and bedtime. We found that our children memorized massive portions of scripture without even trying, especially ones who didn't fall asleep right away. At one point, eight-year-old Josh could finish any verse in Matthew that you began.

Recently when Rick was reading the Proverb of the day for family devotions (there are thirty-one proverbs – read the first chapter on the first day of the month, etc.), Tucker, then nine, would finish every verse Rick started to read. Rick asked him how he knew them all and he said he was listening to "Uncle Rick Reads the Proverbs" at naptime.

Scripture is something you take with you to heaven and through eternity. It never returns void. It seems to just pop into your head when you need it. We offer the tapes Rick made for our kids, or you can make them for your own kids, or buy the Bible on tape; but please consider using them. As our kids grow beyond "nap" stage, Mom still needs a quiet time each day, and so do they. We allow them to play quietly in their rooms and listen to Bible tapes. We also use them for long trips in the car. You can even let them use their own walkmans for times where they have long waits in the doctor's office, etc.

Joshua 1:8 promises that we will be successful in everything we do if we meditate on God's Word. That's what I want for my children. An added benefit is that our children have had very little problem with nightmares. They go to sleep listening to God's Word, and it acts as a purifier and fills their minds with truth as they drift off to sleep. So crank up those CD players and let God's Word make your little ones into mighty soldiers for the King!

 Chapter Seven

Guard Their Hearts

God has entrusted us with the awesome responsibility of raising His children. Wow! A major responsibility we have as parents is to guard their hearts – to protect them. If we don't do it, who will? We will answer to God for how we protected the charge He entrusted to us. It's up to us, not the church, not the government, not the community.

We live in a period of history when we need to constantly be on guard. God tells us in Romans 16:9, "I want you to be wise about what is good, and innocent about what is evil." We are not to learn details of evil just to know it's wrong or to somehow think we can minister to others better. It's not God's way.

Proverbs 13:20 says that the companion of fools will suffer harm. Instead we need to guard our children not only against bad friends, but also bad characters in books or on TV. We tend to empathize with characters in books or on TV shows.

We have not had a TV since we were married 31 years

ago. This past Mother's Day, the kids made me a scrapbook and each child wrote something next to their picture. Here's what Nate wrote: "Thanks for putting so many years into raising us. I'm glad you didn't have a TV in the house when we were growing up. Thanks for staying home with us instead of going off to work. You are the best." Your kids probably won't understand when they're young, but they'll thank you for it, when they're older!

There is so much garbage on TV. If you have one, you will have to super-screen it. Even commercials stink. I can't believe the difference when I see something on TV now. It has fallen so far so fast, even from when I was a kid. Beware of "harmless" kid's cartoons that aren't so harmless anymore. Watch for undertones of New Age philosophy and even Satanism. TV shows used to have families with two parents and respectful kids, and right always won in the end. Not anymore. I don't believe you can raise kids to be the best they can be without severely limiting, if not doing away with, TV.

Even if the show is not *bad,* TV stifles creativity. It's so much easier to sit and watch something than to get up and create something or read something. It deadens our sensitivity to right and wrong. Someone once discovered that if a frog is placed in cool water and the water temperature gradually goes up, the frog will boil alive because it never notices the water becoming hot. So it is with TV. We get desensitized to seeing evil. Psalm 101:3 says, "I will set no wicked thing before my eyes."

As of about five years ago, we now have a TV just for video watching, but we still must be careful. Certainly don't allow "second-rate" movies in your home, and don't use the TV as a babysitter, even with educational videos. Use it sparingly.

Encourage your children to read. We try to go to the library on a regular basis and come away with piles of books. Screen your child's reading material. Obviously you can't read every book before they do, but I have the kids choose their books and then I approve them before we check them out. We encourage our kids to run everything they read by scripture and show us anything that doesn't pass the test. Teach them to be discriminating readers and not believe every word they read.

Beware of overuse of electronic entertainment. Kids need time to think, read, write, create and explore.

As for other kids, we have a policy that neighbor kids have to knock on the door to ask if they can play. If we allow our kids to play with them, it's in our yard, and we often will say no. We occasionally invite neighborhood kids to come to our house to make a fabric crayon tee shirt with a Bible verse on it, or a plaque with their name and its meaning. We plan for it before they come, and prepare to minister to them. Once our sons planned a neighborhood party and assigned different snacks for each child to bring. Then Rick, our oldest, shared the gospel with them.

Josh used to play basketball with some of the kids and witnessed to them and prayed for them. A couple of them professed salvation through the years.

At Christmastime, we've made it a tradition to reach out to the neighbors by bringing them a batch of Nativity sugar cookies along with a gospel tract. A few different years we have delivered gifts of Bibles or "Read N Grow" picture bibles to neighborhood kids. We wanted to reach out to them to let them know we cared about them, but not to compromise what we were trying to accomplish in our own kids' lives.

You also need to exercise caution with toys. Beware of fads in toys – superheroes, weird creatures, fantasy characters. Educational toys are ideal, or toys that allow children to act out real situations. Our little girls have lots of dolls. We want to encourage them to love children.

We have steered clear of Barbie dolls for our girls. Barbie exemplifies a "perfect" physique, etc. Instead, we have thoroughly enjoyed Ginny dolls. My sisters used to own them years ago. Ginny dolls are made by Vogue. They are little girl dolls that actually appreciate in value, as Vogue makes only so many before discontinuing that style and make. My girls have several Ginny dolls each with clothes to act out different seasons and situations. One of my sons made them a dollhouse specially made to fit Ginny.

Blocks, learning puzzles, games, trucks, legos, animals; toys that are wholesome - that's what to look for.

Let me add one note here. Expect differences between little boys and little girls. Those differences are God-designed, and require real parental discretion to understand.

It's easy for us Moms to encourage our little girls to play with dolls to develop those nurturing tendencies of a Mommy. It's a bit harder, though, to come to grips with our responsibility to train our sons to develop their God-given responsibility to be a defender of the weaker sex.

In the early days of my parenting experience, I bought

into the theory that "violence" in any form is wrong and when my four older boys were little toy guns had no place in our home. Through the years, though, I came to realize the many deficiencies with that line of thinking. First of all, the Bible recounts lots of situations of violence, but with God's wisdom behind it all.

It is absurd to expect our sons to be the defenders of their wives and children, and yet discourage or even punish them for exhibiting the very traits necessary to develop the skills for protecting others. Let me clarify that we must teach our sons the difference between fighting for a righteous cause and wanton violence for selfish purposes. We must instill in them a strong and careful sense of justice and emphasize personal responsibility and an understanding of the fact that there are serious consequences for our actions.

God has ordained the differences in men and women for a reason. As a wife and Mom, isn't one of the reasons that our husbands are a tower of strength for us, the fact that we know, if we were to hear a disturbing noise in the middle of the night, that he would be the one to grab a handgun or baseball bat and check it out? Certainly we wouldn't prefer that he leave it up to us or just cower fearfully in indecision.

Rest assured, if we teach our sons justice and responsibility we need not fear we will wind up with little cavemen. Teaching respect for God, people, and property will provide the necessary balance. Also, a thorough education in manners and respect for women are civilizing influences that will protect against abuse.

That's why your little boys are drawn to guns when

they see them. Our sons have all had BB guns and were taught strict rules for handling guns, but were encouraged to practice their aim. Tuck, our 11-yr-old, now has his own 20-gauge shotgun and goes hunting each fall with his older brothers who, by the way, have set rules for gun handling. He's hoping to put a deer in our freezer this fall!

Don't make the mistake of squelching the aggressive energy of your sons, but instead learn to harness it and direct it in God-given outlets. For those sons who seemingly have a never-ending supply of energy, don't be afraid to channel it in other productive directions. For instance, such energy could work wonders on that pile of firewood waiting to be split up!!

One other caution is in the area of music. Ultimately all music should glorify God, so we are kind of picky about the types of music we allow our kids to listen to. Even some children's tapes are too "rocky" or "rappy" for us, so we use caution in what we choose.

We periodically do a book check in our house and weed out any unprofitable reading material that may have slipped by us.

Books we read in our childhood always hold a special place in our hearts. Let's make sure we leave our kids with things they can remember and thank God for.

Kids' free time is important. Just be sure that your tools, books, toys, music and entertainments all work together in building mighty servants of God.

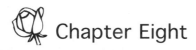 Chapter Eight

*T*urning Problems Into Projects

Our natural tendency is to run from our troubles and hide, or pretend they don't exist. We once heard the illustration given that old lions are the ones that roar and scare their prey. The prey gets frightened and runs away from the roar – only to be eaten by the young lion, waiting to pounce on it. The old lion has no teeth and is not the one to be feared.

So it is, we have found, with our problems. We want to turn and run, whereas God desires that we run toward the source of the conflict and draw on His wisdom to tackle it.

As problems would arise in our family, we soon learned to practice this principle. Instead of getting discouraged, giving up, or trying to ignore a problem, we would run ahead full force and ask God for wisdom to tackle it. Let problems direct your focus. Just as pain alerts us to a problem, conflict alerts us to God's direction for our lives.

That, in actuality, is what our ministry at the Learning Parent has risen from. (We call ourselves the Learning Parent, because the more we learn, the more we realize how much is left to learn.)

I remember Rick coming home from work one day and asking how my day went. Boy, was I frustrated. Rick asked why and I couldn't really put my finger on it, so at his suggestion, over the next couple of days, I wrote a list of everything I got frustrated about. The result was pretty amazing. It wasn't hundreds of things, as it had seemed, just several things that kept occurring over and over again. Hmm – that seemed less overwhelming already. Rick helped me evaluate each one and come up with a project for handling it. In one case I found I just needed another bookcase.

Also we isolated a couple of character deficiencies in the kids, so we made a chart to help our kids realize what behavior they needed to work on. For example, our oldest son Rick would walk in the house and holler, "Mom!" at the top of his lungs, sometimes waking the baby I'd just gotten to sleep or just adding to the general confusion. So on the chart, the problem was "HEY MOM!" and the verse was first Corinthians 14:40, "Let all things be done decently and in order. The desired behavior was to go find Mom and then talk to her. Easy, right? He didn't realize what a disruption that one simple act was causing.

Now, imagine you have 14 children. Each one has a pair of church shoes, a pair of play shoes, a pair of going to town shoes, a pair of boots, and a pair of sandals. How many pairs of shoes is that? And what in the world do you do with them when you have average-sized closets and 2-3 children sharing a closet?

Well, that situation may be unique to us, but you've got some unique to you, too. Address them. Find a solution. Make your life easier!

What Rick did was build a big shoe shelf with compartments to hold forty-eight pairs of shoes. We plunked it down in the entryway, and voila! Another huge irritation was resolved!

That's just a couple of our concrete examples. I've got lots more. But let's learn to face the problems – attack them head on and conquer them!

 Chapter Nine

Keeping the Peace

Okay – we all have to deal with this. Usually there's one instigator kid. Our second son Tim, almost from the day he was born, loved to get reactions out of people. I remember him at about eighteen months of age, standing on the edge of the wading pool, slowly letting the water drain out, as big brother Ricky was wildly waving his arms, hollering and screaming. Tim, with the corners of his mouth turned slightly up, was delighted with the response. Tim was a master at figuring out where people's buttons were and pushing them for the desired reactions.

Then there's Nate. It was Tim's job as a teen to wake Nate and get him out of bed in the morning. Tim, the early bird, and Nate, laid back, phlegmatic and definitely a night person, did not cooperate.

And of course, there's the messy child and the neat child. Each one drives the other straight up the wall.

It's time for church. Mom and most of the kids are waiting in the car. Dad and the nameless child are not. Every week, the same scenario. Some chomping at the bit not wanting to be late, and others totally oblivious and painfully slow.

What do you do? How do you manage without driving each other bonkers? One thing is for sure - Family is the training ground for learning how to get along with lots of different people. God has a great sense of humor and He never makes mistakes. He knew just which character tendencies to give each child and each parent. His will is for each of us to learn from one another – to cooperate together to accomplish a mission for Him. Very often, the trial of getting along with a brother or sister is the very training that God ordained to fully equip each one for God's plan for eternity.

Little things can help. For instance, if two children are sharing a piece of cake, let one cut it and the other choose which "half" they want. Try to put two "messies" in a room together and reward a "clean freak" to show the others step by step how to clean a room. As much as possible, create a place for everything. For young children, put pictures on the boxes for matchbox cars or dollhouse people.

On a periodic basis, I do what I call "room check". If someone's room is clean enough to pass inspection, they get a treat, a few fun-size candy bars, on their bed. If not, they don't get the treat. Sometimes I give them a little warning, but I don't tell them exactly when I'll do it. (They learned to check the grocery bags to see if there was candy; if there was, they'd alert the others, "Hey, Mom's about to do a room check"). But hey, it works!

Reward good habits. When we saw that table manners needed improving, we gave some extra instruction and promised a trip out to eat for two weeks worth of good manners. This shows them that it really is possible to do it!

Usually when someone's behavior really irritates us, it reveals something about our own character that we need to deal with. Mom and Dad have to put on the role of coach sometimes and come alongside each child and walk them through struggles they're facing.

As your kids get older, they will have fun times remembering the irritation of trying to get along with siblings and laugh. Each learns when to give and take, and can become a master at human relations. I recall my oldest son at about three years of age demonstrating his psychology with his younger brother who was trying to knock over Rick's stack of blocks. Rickey quickly got another toy, showed it to Tim, and pretended to be delighted with it. Tim forgot about knocking down the blocks and went for the toy. It worked!

If two children are having trouble getting along, one thing I have often done is a principle illustrated in Matthew 6:21: "Where your treasure is, there will your heart be also." Come alongside each one separately and explain this scripture to them. Then encourage them to prepare a "surprise" for the other child. It's a secret just you and your child know about. Help them to do or make something nice for the other child. Do it with both children and soon you'll see that God's Word does have the answers. As they invest their time and energy in planning secret surprises for the other child, their heart will begin to turn toward them.

It's against our nature to reward evil with good, but isn't that God's way? In Matthew 5:44, God's Word lays out a plan for us to follow when we are offended: "But I say unto you, love your enemies, bless them that curse you, do good to them that hate you, and pray for them that despitefully use you and persecute you..."

This is the very plan we must implement within our families. God's Word tells us how to handle offenses and He will bless our obedience to His Word. Try to record instances of God's supernatural working in your life and your children's lives as they implement His plan and reap His rewards.

Chapter Ten

It All Started In The Bathtub

We all have our favorite places to talk. For us, most of our major brainstorms come about either when we go out to eat, or when Rick is in the bathtub. The latter was the setting for our branching out on our home schooling adventure.

Rick was taking one of his LONG soaks in the tub after a hard day of physical work. I had something on my mind, and so invaded his peaceful surroundings.

The year was 1980. At the time, we had four little boys five years old and under, with Katie, our first daughter, on the way. We had our two oldest boys enrolled in an excellent Christian preschool at our church. They focused on character training and we loved the teachers, but I had a major problem with the whole thing. We lived 40 minutes from the church in the quiet little town of Concord, Virginia.

I had always scheduled my days with the boys so as to teach them scripture and character and just spend time with them. Our preschool adventure was a total disruption. It consisted of only three days a week, but involved well over an hour of driving time each day. I was pleased with what Rick and Tim were learning, but my heart was also torn for Nate and Josh, my two babies, who, instead of having time with Mom, were being hauled back and forth in their car seats for two hours each day. If I stayed in town killing time until preschool was over, it just wasn't valuable time with them.

One day, I did stay and peek in at what went on in preschool. It was great. But God sent the message crashing down upon me, "Hey, you can do this – at home – with all four of your little ones." Yes, I could. I wanted to. I'd love it! Perfect solution!

So that's where the bathtub comes in. I made my case to Rick, who agreed, skeptically at first, to my suggestion to teach Rickey kindergarten at home the next year. We'd never heard of teaching your own kids at home. Rick finally said, "I know you can do it. It's only kindergarten, right?"

We then went to the principal of our Christian school and presented our plan to him. He was supportive – for kindergarten – and showed us materials they used in our school, A Beka Books.

It looked fun. I was excited. The next couple of months were spent setting up a "classroom" in the basement, complete with a chalkboard, bulletin board, school table and chairs, maps, globes, etc. (We later discovered it's not *necessary* to have all that stuff!)

The boys were excited. We hung up pictures from Ideals magazines on the walls, the boys helped me make character quality bulletin boards to teach from, we stocked up on supplies, hung ABC's around the wall, ordered books, and we were ready to fly!

It was a fun first year. Little Rickey not only completed kindergarten, but first grade as well, Tim learned all his sounds and was ready to read, and well – the rest is history. We decided then and there that school was not the place for our boys; home was, and their progress and love for learning was incredible. Little Nate and Josh were learning, too.

It's hard to describe the sensation of watching your child stumble through phonics and finally make sense of it all, trying to fill that unquenchable desire to read, watching them grasp a new concept and then saying, "Oh, now I see. It's easy" – watching individual interests creep up, and you, the parent, just supplying books and materials to explore them ... there's nothing quite like it. I wouldn't trade my years teaching my kids at home for anything.

Everything was hunky dory – until we moved! It's true, we never heard of anyone else doing what we were doing. Presumably a new neighbor had never heard of such a thing either. It probably didn't help that we had bought a house that had had a fire, and we were fixing it up. It ended up being a great investment, but of course it took longer than we anticipated, and it was far from complete when we moved in.

Then it happened. One day in late October we had a knock on our door. It was a truant officer, and apparently he hadn't heard of home education either. Well, he threatened all sorts of things, like taking our kids away, etc., and kept us in suspense for a couple of weeks before we were seeing papers with a truancy charge.

The fear and desperation we felt are hard to convey. This was back in the days before there was an HSLDA (Home School Legal Defense Association), which, by the way, every home schooling family ought to join with a gratefulness for all the watchful care and protection they now afford all home schoolers. John Whitehead had just founded the brand-new Rutherford Institute, but was working out of his basement on a limited budget and couldn't help, but he told us of a constitutional lawyer friend of his, Steve Graber, whom we ended up employing to represent us.

Steve came to our home, watched me conduct school with my children, documented everything, and researched the law. Virginia law granted us the right to teach our children under the religious exemption clause. He put in an enormous amount of preparation and finally court day came in December of 1982.

That day opened my eyes to the decline of our judicial system in this country. We had a judge - the cousin of the truant officer, by the way - who sat arrogantly behind his desk, with his feet on the desk in front of him, and did not permit our lawyer to say anything about religion. Mr. Graber informed him that it was the religious exemption statute of the Virginia code under which we were pleading our case. He wouldn't hear it – anything. Steve's hours of work went unheard. The judge simply said, "I don't want to hear anything about religion. Put your kids in school." That was it. Case closed. We were fined and told to put our kids in school.

By the way, today we are home educating our children under the same religious exemption statute. The state hasn't changed the wording since the 1970's. It's not that the state of Virginia didn't give us the right, it's that the judge wouldn't even listen to the law being read. We were devastated! We were ready to move, whatever it took. We could appeal, but funds weren't available for that and Steve advised us that if we did appeal, we HAD to win – precedents were being set.

It's hard to describe what it felt like. We had a few wonderful friends who stuck by us, but by and large, the whole Christian world turned its back. The Christian school movement was growing, and Christians couldn't understand why we didn't put our kids in a Christian school.

The answer to that was that we had a super-strong burden from the Lord that we must home educate our children. We had a conviction that we were willing to die for, although we probably couldn't logically explain why until years later, when we discovered that God branded it on our hearts and on the hearts of other parents all across the country. We didn't know each other existed at the time. We had no clue at all that God was there on the cutting edge of a gigantic movement that was going to sweep across our country and I believe, reclaim our country for God. All we knew was that God had given us such a strong passion for training our children, and the path was clear. It wasn't easy, but it was clear, and we knew we had to take it.

We tried to sell our house, but who wants a house that's not totally fixed up from fire damage? We did put it on the market and showed it several times.

I distinctly remember the day the door bell rang and a lady had come to the house. We normally showed it by appointment only, but she was insistent. Well, the kids had been drilled and knew what to do. If anyone came to the door during school hours, they had to climb under their beds and be perfectly quiet and still. They did. It was when I was showing the woman Nate's room that I noticed the slippers. You remember – those big fuzzy animal slippers? Well, Nate had a pair on, and he was under his bed like he was told, but his slippers hadn't quite made it. There they were, sticking straight up in the air, as if hanging in mid-air. I quickly whisked her on to the next room, hoping desperately that she hadn't noticed the strange slippers mysteriously hung in space.

Well, to make a long story short, we eventually worked out an arrangement with our little church school. They let us enroll our children in their school, only I was their teacher. I would get up early every morning, get my five little munchkins ready, and we'd take off for our school day away from home. It was a tremendous relief for me to be able to continue teaching my children. We had a little kerosene heater for our room, and to this day, I feel sick all over again whenever I smell kerosene.

The following year we helped lobby for new legislation in Richmond, and feeling certain that it would pass, we again stayed at home, this time with closed curtains. The legislation did pass in January, so although religious reasons were still our reason for home educating, we complied with a new statute and notified our superintendent, certifying that our curriculum covered the

Virginia standard of learning objectives, and then having our kids tested yearly with a standardized test – we chose IOWA Basic.

After many years of excellent test results, we again filed for religious exemption and it was recognized, but as I said, the clause in the law never changed in wording since the 1970's.

Home educating our children is a decision I have never regretted. I'm glad we stuck it out when the going was tough. It's the best thing we could have done for our kids, and God's hand of blessing was on it.

 Chapter Eleven

Keep It Simple – Home Education At Its Best

Home education is not complicated. It requires dedication on your part, and diligence, but it's not complicated. Beware of curricula that try to make it so. We've found it's not so much what curriculum you use, as it's how you use it. Home education should be a discipleship process, taking your children by the hand and walking through life with them. Our goal is to prepare spiritually strong adults. Whatever you need to learn, they do too.

Academics takes us about two and a half to three hours a day. You've got to be there with the kids. It doesn't work to say, "Go do your schoolwork." I am in the same room with my kids, assigning their work, showing them the next concept, answering their questions and being available to help if they need it.

Most curricula are just too full of busywork. For instance, in math, I will circle eight to twelve problems a day. If it's a new concept, I explain it, let them watch me do one, watch them do one, and then let them go finish, being available if they get stuck. Then I correct the work as soon as they finish and let them make any corrections needed.

There isn't any point in having them do thirty problems if they understand twelve. If they master it, we go on the next day. If not, we stay there until they master it. If you give them too much to do, they'll get discouraged. For younger children, I let them answer questions orally as much as possible. I do require them to do a small amount of handwriting each day, and do it neatly, but if you give them too much to write, they'll just try to get it done and not care about accuracy.

Along about 3rd grade we start spelling and language. Until then, we focus first on phonics and then reading, so they get a good foundation in reading. Many language programs in earlier grades spend a lot of time teaching concepts much more easily understood after the child has become proficient in reading. For example, many will have children copy whole sentences just to put a capital letter at the beginning and a period at the end. If you just wait until 3rd grade, they've seen it again and again and learning to do that comes naturally.

By about the second or third grade, we start spelling. Often by then, you can tell whether or not a child will be a good speller or have difficulty. Once a child has mastered spelling and is getting all the words correct, we start vocabulary about 7th grade and no longer do spelling, except for occasional spelling bees just for fun.

For history, science, and health I just let each child

read on their own level. We supplement a lot with excellent resources. I read to the younger ones often, as does Rick.

I have a ten-year-old who absolutely loves science, so we often do science experiments. I've used books that use simple, everyday items to illustrate science concepts. It's his favorite part of the day.

I have discovered a wonderful line of early reading books. I try to use readers that teach Bible, nature or history instead of using "silly" readers. I've found that children catch onto reading better when they are reading something that is interesting and makes sense.

We've found that field trips usually make a lot more sense for one family than for several families to go in a group. The parents are available to actually teach the children and the children aren't distracted by being with a bunch of other kids. There are exceptions, like going to a planetarium or somewhere that you need a big group, but the family unit is definitely our preference for the most effective learning experience.

I've also found that preschoolers and those I'm teaching to read take the biggest time involvement for me. Once your child gets to a high school level, they ought to be a self-directed learner. That's why all the colleges are pursuing home educated kids. I pretty much just assign their work and let them go to it. Sometimes high schoolers will have extra reading to finish up in the afternoons, but my time involvement with academics is done by noon.

The degree of success in my home schooling often depends on how I handle my preschoolers. Preschoolers want to be a part of "school." It's a temptation for many people is to send them away to the TV, but try as often as possible to include them in your schooling.

What I would do every summer to get ready for the start of school was prepare a variety of preschool learning activities, reserved solely for "school time." Don't let them use them any other time, and then they will anticipate the fun of school. I use things like learning puzzles. My kids have learned so much through learning puzzles. My son Matt learned his states and capitals at a very early age just by doing USA puzzles. Lace and trace activities are also very good for learning coordination. Shape sorters, blocks, ABC puzzles and books, preschool workbooks, peg play, felt books and magnetic puzzles are all very good.

I also cut shapes from construction paper and let them use glue sticks to stick them to sheets of construction paper. I gather household objects suitable for outlining, such as jar lids, popsicle sticks, etc. My little ones love stickers. I buy special drawing tablets, markers, colored pencils, chunky crayons, etc., and earmark them for school time. I use homemade play dough, complete with rolling pins, molds, plastic knives, etc., that keeps their attention for long periods of time.

Each toddler has different lengths of attention spans, so they all differ, but the key is to have plenty of activities and change them while they're still interested in them. Then they will be looking forward to doing them another day. I also let little ones play quietly in the school room with dollhouse or farm sets. Little guys have to learn to use "school time voices" and older ones have to learn to concentrate without complete silence. It just never happens!

If older ones are working on something that requires extra concentration, they can go to their room to read. Normally though, we use our kitchen table for little ones' preschool activities, the dining room table for writing, and the living room for reading.

It's not easy. Some kids are more trying than others. Take heart, though. Six months' time makes a lot of difference. It's those fifteen-month to two-and-a-half-year-olds that are the hardest to manage usually, but by next school year, what a difference you'll see!

Let your older ones know it's important for little ones to be learning also, and you'll be amazed at the amount of academics they actually learn just from being present. I remember Josh's dismay one day as his two-year-old sister piped up with the answer to nine times four. She'd just heard me drilling him in a sing-song manner, and she remembered it!

Things put to music are easily remembered. I made up a little tune for helping and being verbs, and all the kids remember them to this day, even though they're not impressed with their mother's musical genius.

If you teach your children how to read and how to enjoy learning and how to research, you've done your job. Life is a continual learning process. Don't feel like you have to know everything and then spout it off to your children. Children often learn better by observing mom learn something new. My kids have a much better education than I did.

Much of the work is already done for you if you just provide good learning materials and watch learning naturally happen. When a child develops an interest, pursue it. Go to the library, get books, supplies, info, whatever, to help them learn. Our whole family learned all about rabbits when Nate developed an interest in them. Growing up, he had several rabbits and studied all about them.

When Rick became involved in politics, we all learned so much more than I ever dreamed. We became a grassroots team this past year to help campaign when he ran for supervisor in his county. God gives the interests and passions, and we supply information and legwork. God grows us in wisdom.

Expand your kids' horizons by simple things. Leave a book lying around the house somewhere and see if the kids pick it up and read it. Subscribe to Christian news, nature and history magazines and watch learning happen. Try to have a reading night with snacks, instead of watching movies. Rick will often read a classic or adventure novel or historical story to the kids.

Bible quiz nights are another big hit at our house. We'll get a bag of candy for rewards and give age-appropriate Bible questions starting from youngest to oldest. If someone can't answer a question, the next oldest will try until someone gets it. Usually the child who missed will get an easier question. It really gives them motivation to concentrate and pay attention to Bible stories.

You can do it! You don't need video courses, charter schools or satellite schools. Your kids need you. That's why you're home educating, right? That's what it's all about. God gave your kids to you. He'll equip you to guide them in their learning process. There's something really special about the parent-child relationship. Don't miss out on it. After all, God is omnipotent and all His wisdom is available to you just for the asking. Your kids belong to Him and He's waiting to pour out his wisdom on you (Prov. 8:17, "I love them that love me; and them that seek me early shall find me").

 Chapter Twelve

Standing Alone

Through the years, we've found ourselves standing alone a lot of the time, and you probably will do the same. We home educated our children, we had a large family, we had four of our kids at home, we kept our kids with us in church instead of sending them to Sunday school, youth groups, children's church and AWANA programs. We never had a TV, there were toys and games and books we wouldn't let our children have. You might say we stuck out like a sore thumb.

Ultimately though, we as parents will answer to God for how we've reared our children - not the school teachers, not the church, not the youth pastors. As God impresses conviction on our hearts for how He wants us to rear His children, we must be willing to put up with the flak we receive from others. If we remain steadfast to one conviction, God builds into us an important beatitude – "Blessed are those which are persecuted for righteousness' sake, for theirs is the kingdom of heaven" (Matt. 5:10).

God has to take us through trials to make us strong. Many of the stands we had to take were relatively unheard of at the time and we had no evidence that we were right, just a conviction from God. As far as home education goes, it's now fact - parents can now get concrete information as to the success rate of home educated kids who are now young adults.

Ask God to give you convictions as to what He wants you to do, and remain true to them. When we started home educating, the only thing that kept us going was conviction. It's so much clearer now, but my caution to you would be don't lose sight of your conviction. Don't be lured into "watered-down" home schooling; don't let promises of free computers or anything else cause you to compromise on what and how you teach your children.

The world doesn't have the answers; God does. Teach your children solid truth. Kids don't need exposure to wrong. Chinese bankers used to let their children play with real money. They were then quick to recognize the counterfeit. So it is with truth - they'll be quick to discern untruth or wrong. Romans 16:19 cautions us to be innocent of evil, but wise in what is good. That should be our measuring stick for what we teach our children.

Why is it that we automatically assume that the way it's done in schools and churches is the best way for our kids? Why not, instead, be quick to turn to scripture and see what God has to say for training children? It's hard to always be doing things in a different way than most folks do things. But look around you. Do you really want your kids to fit in with today's world? God's way down through the ages has never made sense to the world. The road of least opposition is generally not God's way.

What we found to be true in the life of our family was that we were called to take a lot of unpopular stands.

Often, other Christians would think we were nuts, although we never tried to impose our convictions on them. We'd get flak, we'd rely all the more on God, He'd strengthen and encourage us, and years later those very people that thought we were nuts would end up respecting us and our family. Although the respect of others is not our goal, pleasing God is. But as our children were becoming adults and people saw fruit in their lives, they would often end up respecting us for how we raised our children.

People always feel threatened when you do things really differently from the mainstream. But we must remember we're trying to please God, not men.

It was always tough for me to announce to others that I was expecting again. Not very many people consider children to be a blessing and it wasn't easy to just let all the rude comments roll off your back. Somewhere about child number seven or eight, God gave me these special verses, I Peter 4:14,16, 19. It's a great passage to read when everyone thinks you're crazy.

The insights God showed me were first of all, what am I having trouble responding to? The answer? People being insulted at my letting God be in control of my life in the area of childbearing. The tendency of people is to feel ashamed, or at least hesitant to share your 'good news' with others.

The godly response involved four parts:
Do not be ashamed.
Praise God that I bear His Name.
Commit myself anew to my Creator (this is a crucial step)
Continue to do good (what I know to be the right course

for me).

And here comes the best part – God's blessing. Verse fourteen tells us the Spirit of the glory of God will rest upon you and give you that extra special grace. Grace is the desire *and* power to do God's will.

There you have it – the answer is so clear in God's Word. It's been a tremendous encouragement to me over the years.

It was also hard explaining to others, especially family members, why we didn't let our kids play with certain toys like Barbie dolls, read fairy tales, watch TV, etc. But I found that usually people weren't really interested in why. They just wanted to put you down so they wouldn't have to deal with the fact that maybe you were right.

Occasionally, a young mom or dad really was interested in why we did things the way we did them, and then of course we'd explain as best we could. But generally, I'd just give a short, kind answer and let it go at that, and they'd usually drop it. I never felt it was my mission to try to convert others to my beliefs or waste my time giving in-depth explanations to those who weren't really listening (don't throw pearls before swine).

God leads different people on different paths and gives them convictions at different times in their lives. So don't feel like you have to convince others, but on the other hand, don't let pressure from others weaken convictions God has placed on your heart for your children. As you stand firm, God will build character in you and your children.

My son Rick wrote this article when he was opinion editor for the school paper at Liberty University:

"It's not Thanksgiving yet, but I have something to be thankful for, so I'll jump the gun a bit.

I reflect back on some lessons I learned from my parents. Some they taught me by rote, some by example. (Unfortunately, Mom will probably read my finished column before I do, so she's bound to think I'm currying favor. I'm not, though a fresh batch of chocolate chip cookies would be nice.

Let me just list a few of these lessons for the reader's consideration.

While I have flunked in this area lately, I'm thankful for my mom's early encouragement to memorize Scripture. My spiritual condition today, such as it is, is largely due to this. Almost by the time I learned to talk, I knew many Bible verses. I used to win all the Bible Trivia games. More importantly, I have a store of God's written Word where I can easily get it. Thanks, mom!

2.   My dad taught me the same lesson Abe Lincoln's father taught him. He said once, "My father taught me to work, but he never taught me to like it." I still don't like to work; I reckon I never will. Yet I know the value of work now. I feel much better when I'm doing something productive. I like the feeling of coming home at the end of the day exhausted but satisfied. I still wouldn't do it if I didn't get paid, but...

I have no idea if I've learned this lesson yet; at this rate I'll never know. But my parents showed me how to make a marriage work. I'm sure they disagreed on occasion, but I've never seen them argue in front of me, much less fight.

They taught me the value of church. As a kid I hated it. Church was a decided impediment to my weekend. I preferred to play all day. After all, how could I go through the agony of getting all dressed up on God's prescribed day of rest?

Now though, I'm at church every time the doors are open. I love to have a part in the service; I love to be a part of the praise. When I have to miss a service, or God forbid, two in a row, I miss everybody. Church feels like family. I get my spiritual batteries recharged on Sundays and Wednesdays.

This is one lesson I'm glad I had to learn. It's always been understood in my family that such vices as alcohol and tobacco are taboo. I've never tried either (although I love inhaling wood smoke). Alcohol has destroyed enough lives and broken families already, and enough smokers have coughed their lives away with lung cancer. I don't want to be a statistic.

My parents have taught me (mostly through bitter necessity) the value of financial frugality. Mt mom can stretch a dollar "till Washington screams," as Dad says. They've taught me (through mistakes!) the danger of debt. I still don't have a credit card and my station wagon, rugged though it is, is paid for.

I've learned not to jump at the first opportunity; to prioritize what things are important enough to spend my money on. This should come in handy if I have any left after the business office gets their cut.

Last but not least, my parents taught me how to stand alone; how to stand up for what's right when others (even fellow Christians) don't share my convictions.

This is one of those lessons they taught by example. I remember when they first came up with the wacky idea of home schooling. We were the odd men out (maybe we still are!). Virginia law didn't look very kindly on such strange practices, and my parents found themselves in court in defense of what they felt God had directed them to do. Our church, in fact all the churches of Lynchburg, were deafeningly silent: after all, their Christian schools weren't under attack; why bother? Only one family stood with us, yet my parents, in defiance of a court order, continued to do what they felt was right. They were scared to death, to be sure (to this day my mom cringes at the sound of police sirens), but they continued in the face of the might of the Commonwealth of Virginia. In 1982 the law was liberalized, making their choice legal and reducing the persecution.

I find that I don't scare easily; if I see something as right, more often than not I'll fight for it no matter what. Whether or not it's popular with the world, or even with fellow Christians, I've found the strength to stand alone. I'm so thankful that my parents practiced Daniel's creed. They "purposed in their hearts" to do what they felt was right. I'll never forget it.

God promises in Isaiah 58 that those who stand for what's right will "raise up the foundations of many generations." My parents have taught the next generation the meaning of commitment, of principle."

When God takes your family through trials, cooperate with Him in it, stand firm, and God will use it to be a part of your life message, and that of your children.

My older boys, the ones who used to hide under the bed, have a deep passion for seeing America return to it's godly roots and principles. I asked Rick once, what did you think about back when you were hiding under the bed? He said, "This shouldn't be happening, not in the United States of America." And it shouldn't have, but God used that incredibly tough time in our lives to equip and empower our children with a godly burden to be used to help inform others and elect godly people to again rule our country by God's principles.

 Chapter Thirteen

Building Patriot's Hearts

Our family has, through the leadership of my oldest son, become very actively involved in grassroots politics. Did you know that to be elected to office in the U.S. at the time of the founders and well beyond, that you had to ascribe to the Christian faith? John Adams, our second president, declared that our republican form of government was established for a religious and moral people and was "wholly inadequate to the government of any other." Even the original state constitutions reflect the spiritual temperature of America.

Here are a couple of examples:

Delaware - "Every person appointed to public office shall say, 'I do profess belief in God, the Father, and in Jesus Christ, His only Son, and in the Holy Ghost, one God, blessed forevermore, and I do acknowledge the holy scriptures of the Old and New Testaments to be given by divine inspiration.'"

Pennsylvania and **Vermont** – "And each member [of the legislature] before he takes his seat, shall make and subscribe the following declaration, 'I do believe in one God, the Creator and Governor of the universe, the rewarder of the good and the punisher of the wicked.'"

The Founders, through the state constitutions, were ensuring that legislators would acknowledge that when they left office, they would be accountable for their actions while in office, not only to the voters, but to God. I didn't know that. I was educated in our public school system and the only two founders I learned anything about were Thomas Jefferson and Benjamin Franklin, two of the least religious of our founders. But even Ben Franklin feared God. He said, "If a sparrow cannot fall to the ground without His notice, is it probable that an empire can rise without His aid?" He also called for regular prayer to make sure we kept God in the middle of our nation's business.

Thomas Jefferson declared the Bible and Isaac Watts' hymnals as the official school textbooks used in Washington's public schools.

Did you know that about ninety-five percent of our founders were, by their own words, "unashamedly Christian"? Listen to what they had to say:

Samuel Adams – "I rely upon the merits of Jesus Christ for a pardon of all my sins."

Charles Carroll – "On the mercy of my Redeemer I rely for salvation and on His merits; not on the works I have done in obedience to His precepts."

John Witherspoon – "I entreat you in the most earnest manner to believe in Jesus Christ, for there is no salvation in any other."

Robert Treat Paine – "I am constrained to express my

adoration of ... the Author of my existence, in full belief of ... His forgiving mercy revealed to the world through Jesus Christ, through whom I hope for never ending happiness in a future state."

Benjamin Rush – "My only hope of salvation is in the infinite, transcendent love of God manifested to the world by the death of His Son upon the cross. Nothing but His blood will wash away my sins. I rely exclusively upon it. Come, Lord Jesus. Come quickly!"

Roger Sherman – "I believe that there is only one living and true God, existing in three persons, the Father, the Son, and the Holy Ghost ... and that at the end of this world, there will be a resurrection of the dead, and a final judgment of all mankind, when the righteous shall be publicly acquitted before Christ the Judge, and be admitted to everlasting life and glory, and the wicked be sentenced to everlasting punishment."

Gunning Bedford – "To the triune God - the Father, the Son, and the Holy Ghost - be ascribed all honor and dominion forever more. Amen."

John Jay – "Unto Him Who is the author and giver of all good, I render sincere and humble thanks for His manifold and unmerited blessings, and especially for our redemption and salvation by His beloved Son ... Blessed be His holy Name."

That's just a few. It's astounding. Is there any doubt that we in fact do have a godly heritage! Praise God!

When a state applied for statehood, they had to affirm in their state constitution that they would teach the Christian religion in their public schools, or they would be denied entrance into the United States. Patrick Henry, remembered best for being the powerful orator of the "give me liberty or give me death" speech, once stated, "It cannot be emphasized too strongly or too often that this great nation was founded, not by religionists, but by Christians, not on religion, but on the gospel of Jesus Christ."

John Quincy Adams, our sixth president, said, "The highest glory of the American Revolution was this ... it connected in one indissoluble bond the principles of civil government with the principles of Christianity."

Our family has been truly blessed and educated by watching David Barton (Wallbuilders Ministries) video tapes together. We've rediscovered so many exciting truths of the Christian founding and basis for our form of government. Did you know the founders used scripture as a model for our government?

For example:

Separation of powers – Jeremiah 17:

Tax exemption for churches – Ezra 7:24: "Also we certify you, that, touching any of the priests and Levites, singers, porters, Nethinim, or ministers of this house of God, it shall not be lawful to impose toll, tribute, or custom upon them."

Capital Punishment – Deuteronomy 17:6: "At the mouth of two witnesses, or three witnesses, shall he that is worthy of death be put to death; but at the mouth of one witness he shall not be put to death."

Federal, State, County Branches – Isaiah 33:22: "For the Lord is our judge [judicial], the Lord is our lawgiver [legislative], the Lord is our king [executive]; He will save us."

George Washington, in regard to the separation of powers, noted in his farewell address: "A just estimate of that love of power and proneness to abuse it, which predominates the human heart, is sufficient to satisfy us of the truth of this position. The necessity of checks in the exercise of political power by dividing and distributing depositories ... has been established."

Our godly heritage as a nation has been neglected and almost forgotten. If we don't understand our freedoms, we won't recognize when we are about to lose them. I believe it is our duty to rediscover these truths and teach them to our children. After we watched Barton's video series, our kids invited friends over and Monday nights became our night to inform our friends. Our kids then suggested to our church leaders that Rick and I moderate a class, showing the Barton videos and discussing them. We are now on our second 12-week series of doing just that.

It has been so exciting to hear people's exclamations when hearing, many for the first time, that our form of government has its roots in scripture. Our founders were largely dedicated, committed Christian men. Abigail Adams said, "I cannot conceive that a man could claim to be a patriot who is not first a Christian."

When our founders signed the Declaration of Independence, they really were committing their lives, fortune, and honor; those weren't empty words. King George gave orders to find and kill all the signers. Many had to flee, leave families, or go into hiding.

Robert Morris, a founder, financed the Revolution out of his own pocket – two million dollars. He was never repaid, never complained, and spent his final days in debtor's prison.

John Hancock from Boston was a wealthy merchant. He had to flee for his life. The British confiscated his mansion and set up headquarters there in Boston. The people of Boston respected Hancock too much to do anything about it, so when Hancock found out, he gathered up a militia and returned to Boston to burn his own mansion and belongings rather than let the British benefit at American expense.

These are just two of the 250-plus signers. David Barton has reprinted an 1836 text book called "The Lives of the Signers." We must familiarize our children with the lives of our founders and the sacrifices made on behalf of *our* freedom. Freedom is never free.

It's never too early to instill this in our childrens' minds. We found an exciting resource to use with three to twelve-year-olds, called "Take Your Hat Off When the Flag Goes By". I was delighted to find it when my youngest was two years old. She walked around the house singing about George Washington, the Declaration of Independence, the branches of our government, checks and balances, etc. Start when they're young to build those patriot's hearts.

Our kids can and will play a major role in turning this country back to God. Brian Ray did a survey comparing home schooled adults ages eighteen to twenty-five to the general population of the same age group. He found that seventeen percent of the latter were involved in politics, as opposed to seventy percent of home schooled adults.

Our children have the opportunity to be salt and

light, to shine as lights in the midst of our crooked and perverse generation, and effect permanent changes! I have great hopes for America because of home schooled children. We must teach our children that it is their duty to be involved in civil government and pick up the torch our founders left to us. I believe America *can* and *will* again be a godly nation.

Here are some practical things everyone can do: Vote. To vote is the very least you can do. Out of the 60 million people in the US who profess to be born again believers and who go to church at least once a week, only <u>fifteen million</u> vote. And a whopping twenty-four million are not even registered to vote!

Another way Satan has duped us is to tell us we're a minority and our vote won't count. The wonderful news is that we're not the minority. If only Christians would turn out in force to vote for godly candidates, we'd win every time. We've got the numbers! Consider getting voter registration forms and passing them out, encouraging other Christians to vote. America can get back to godly principles, fast. It's only in our generation that we've slipped away.

Write your senator and congressmen. It's been said that one hand-written letter to a senator represents about 20,000 voters. They listen to constituents – they want to get re-elected. Make your voice heard.

Stay informed. Set up an email network to inform family and friends on issues to be prayed about, or to contact representatives about.

Join your local Republican party. Beware – not all

Republicans are conservatives. You can actually be a delegate in your locality, district or state and have a large voice in deciding who your party will choose as their candidate. One person has much influence. Bring your children along – anyone of voting age can be a delegate. If your kids are too young to vote, bring them anyway.

Help work the polls on election day. My kids have been there every election day for years, passing out literature and answering questions. The kids that are too young to vote have influenced others to vote for good candidates just by being informed.

Write letters to your editor. That is the most-read section of a newspaper anyway. Encourage your kids to write, too.

Put up yard signs for godly candidates, knock on doors passing out literature. These are just a few things that anyone can do. It's a wonderful way to train your kids to accept their duty as citizens.

Alexis de Tocqueville came to America from France to find out why the American form of government was such a success. He stated, "I sought for the greatness and genius of America in her commodious harbors and her ample rivers — and it was not there ... in her fertile fields and boundless forests — and it was not there ... in her rich mines and her vast world commerce — and it was not there ... in her democratic Congress and her matchless Constitution — and it was not there. Not until I went into the churches of America and heard her pulpits flame with righteousness did I understand the secret of her genius and power. America is great because she is good, and if America ever ceases to be good, America will cease to be great."

John Adams said, "We have no government armed with power capable of contending with human passions unbridled by morality and religion."

In Jeremiah 6:16 we read, "Thus saith the Lord, Stand ye in the ways, and see, and ask for the old paths, where is the good way, and walk therein, and ye shall find rest for your souls." We must rise up and reclaim America for God. We must encourage our children to be informed and to be salt and light, to be the next godly supreme court justice, or senator, or lawyer.

Edmund Burke, the great British statesman and philosopher, said, "All that is necessary for the triumph of evil is for good men to do nothing."

That is why America is in the mess she's in now, but Jesus left us to occupy until His return. Christians must get involved once again in politics and become the head and not the tail.

Charles Finney, a great preacher in the second Great Awakening, noted, "The Church <u>must</u> take right ground in regard to politics. Politics are a part of religion in such a country as this ... Christians must do their duty to the country as part of their duty to God. God will bless or curse this nation according to the course Christians take in politics."

Far too long Satan has duped Christians and they have believed his lie that to be really spiritual, you ought to be a pastor or missionary, but whatever you do, keep out of the civil arena. He has managed to render Christians ineffective in their society by keeping them within the four walls of their churches.

John Jay, the original Chief Justice of the Supreme Court, and perhaps the most influential writer of the Constitution, stated, "Providence has given to our people the choice of their rulers and it is the duty as well as the privilege and interest of a Christian nation to select and prefer Christians for their rulers."

We have a heritage of godliness. We must take back the ground that good men have given up by doing nothing. We must go back to the old paths, the right ways, to preserve our heritage. Reverend Matthias Barnett in 1803, said this, "Let not your children have reason to curse you for giving up these rights, and prostrating those institutions which your fathers delivered to you."

You and your kids are the hope of America! I believe that with all my heart. May God bless you as you purpose to follow Him with all your hearts so that the tide may be turned and God can bless America!

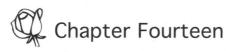 Chapter Fourteen

Building A Heart of Service

Jesus said in Mark 9:35, "If any man desire to be first, the same shall be last of all, and servant of all." We must build a heart of service in each of our children. We can start almost right from the beginning. The family provides a training ground for service. We taught our toddlers to get diapers for baby sister, wash baseboards, throw away trash, etc.

As I run my many errands, I take a different child with me and teach them how to shop and meet the needs of their family, how to put away groceries, weed the garden, keep the yard and house picked up. Each family member needs spheres of responsibility. The family needs each member and each must contribute just as soon as they are able. It's healthy and normal, and children need to know they are needed and valuable to the family unit. Let older children help to train the younger ones in chores, projects, tasks, etc.

I remember when cleaning the bathroom was Nate and Josh's job. I told them when they trained Matt and

Emmy to clean the bathroom thoroughly, then it wouldn't be their job anymore. Talk about motivation! And Matt and Emmy thought it was great to do their older brother's job. Nate and Josh got to learn parenting skills in accurately training their younger siblings to do the job.

Train your kids to serve with responsibility. We have a daily and weekly schedule for chores. Be flexible, but have a schedule, so everyone knows what is expected of them. A schedule builds security.

Certain chores are done on certain days of the week. If it's Monday morning, everyone does their Monday chores. Try to gear the chores according to a child's skill level. Each summer, I reassign chores so everyone will learn all the different chores eventually. Train each child thoroughly in how to do their job. Don't just expect them to know. Do it with them until they become proficient in it and then afterwards, occasionally help them just for motivation.

Make your instructions clear and easy to follow. Some children need more direction than others. For instance, I have one daughter who sees what needs to be done before I do. I have another daughter, however, who is very creative. She just doesn't see the mess! I would walk in her room and she'd be sprawled on her bed writing a story. I'd ask her why she didn't pick up the mess before she wrote stories, and she'd say, "What mess?" She just didn't see it. When dusting was her job, I'd keep finding things that weren't getting dusted. I finally realized she needed help knowing what to dust. So, for handwriting that week, I had her go from room to room and list everything in each room that needed to be dusted. She could then use her list to check things off and make sure she hadn't forgotten anything.

Check up on them. If you don't, they'll try to get away with whatever they think they can. Call them back if the job is not done thoroughly, even if they're already in bed at night when you discover it! Call them back as many times as it takes, and eventually they'll realize they might as well just do it right the first time instead of being interrupted to come and complete jobs.

For spring and fall cleaning, I let up on school work a bit for the week and assign each child extra jobs for each day of the week. It's different from our normal schedule and normally it's kind of fun! We don't pay the kids for doing normal chores. It's just part of belonging to the family. We do, however, pay for extra chores, like cleaning out the shed, washing and cleaning the car, etc. That gives the kids a way to earn extra money. If they need money for something, they'll ask for extra jobs.

Beyond serving as a family member, create projects for service for your child. When we invite company over for dinner, we teach our children to have a servant's spirit and help prepare meals, serve the guests, etc. If other kids come, we assign our kids to watch over one of the visiting kids, watching out for their safety, making sure no one is excluded or picked on, etc., and that rules are followed.

Encourage your children to foster a servant's heart by ministering to their grandparents, or if your parents don't live nearby, as ours don't, consider 'adopting' an elderly person. We've done this with a few elderly people in our church. My daughter Laura has accompanied me each time we visit them and she is a real source of joy in their lives. Train your kids to attentively listen for hints, like their favorite color or flower, foods or books. Then prepare special surprises for them sometimes when you visit. Older people have so much wisdom, and not only will your children be developing servants hearts, but they will be learning wisdom from people they are ministering to.

One of the couples we've 'adopted' is a retired missionary and his wife. He is getting ready to celebrate his 100th birthday this year, and we asked his wife for a list of friends and wrote them letters requesting a picture of themselves and a short remembrance or account of how "Uncle Jim" has blessed their life. We're making an album to put them in for a surprise for his birthday. He has definitely blessed our lives by telling us of his testimony and his life of ministry.

Don't neglect the elderly. It's been said that when an old person dies, a library dies with them. Avail yourself and your children of their years of wisdom at the same time that you are providing a source of joy in the final years of their life.

Children can send school papers and write letters, color pictures, etc., to send to their grandparents or adopted grandparents. We use "A Reason for Writing" handwriting curriculum and each Friday the kids write a Bible verse and color the border sheet around the verse and have a ready-made gift to send to others. It's a much better motivation to write neatly if what they are working on has a purpose and is used to bless someone's life.

We've always encouraged our children to make

homemade gifts for friends, neighbors, brothers and sisters. To think of appropriate gifts and spend time and energy in making a surprise for someone is developing a servant's heart. Rick and I still have plaster of Paris handprints hanging on our walls that the kids made us for Mother's and Father's Day. I had the kids make their dad a tee shirt one year with their hand and footprints all over it, and I wrote Psalm 127:3 on it.

I have kept a sampling over the years of papers, cards and gifts the kids have made us, and I made two huge scrapbooks of some of the extra special ones. They are still very special to me. It almost takes you back to the day you received them to sit and flip through the scrapbook and to appreciate each one.

We were put on this earth to serve. Let us remember to communicate that to our children. We're not here to entertain ourselves, as the world would have us believe. It's only when we empty ourselves into other's lives that we truly find what life is all about!

 Chapter Fifteen

Give Them Your Heart

Mom, Dad, you're the key! This is what I believe is the key to being a good parent – to first of all give God your heart and then give your heart to your children. Kids have to know they have your heart, and you can't fake it! Knowing they have your heart is a safeguard that more often than not will keep them from doing things they know would displease or hurt you.

So just what do I mean by giving them your heart? I mean they have to know you are truly committed to their success – more than you are to your own success. Maybe it would best explain just what I mean by listing some things we as parents are tempted to put above our children.

Our reputation. What will others think? What will my parents think? What will other church members, the neighbors, my friends, think? I see especially in home educators too much concern for what others think because we often have to step out and follow a different tune than most folks. We are tempted to feel like we have to compensate to try to "prove" to others that we're not messing up our children, that our children really are smart, that they really are learning what they're supposed to.

Often we're tempted to over-involve them in extracurricular activities or sports just because that's what everyone thinks you're supposed to do. Could it be that we, who are trying to protect our children from the negative aspects of peer pressure, are succumbing to that very pressure ourselves?

God admonishes us to come out from among them and be separate. We needn't feel like we have to defend what God told us to do. If you have convictions as to how to raise God's children for Him, don't worry about it if others don't understand or approve. As a matter of fact, if everyone approves of what you're doing, maybe that should be a red flag to you to re-evaluate to see if you're really walking God's way!

Our own goals. We grow up with a wish list of what we want to accomplish in our lives, experiences we want to participate in, places we want to go, maybe even material things to accumulate. I'm not saying it is wrong to have goals, but once we have children we need to realize that we might be called to give up some of our own aspirations in order to give ourselves to helping our children accomplish God's plan for their lives.

Instead of trying to interest your child in what delights you, you need to defer to what interests them and be involved. For instance, just because you love to play hockey, don't try to force it on your child. If it's computers or cars or building or animals that delight him, don't fool yourself into believing you're spending quality time with your child dragging him along or worse yet, forcing him to be involved in something he has no desire for.

It's you who has to stretch, give up your goals for now, and become a learning parent. Learn about what delights your child. Just think of what it says to him, not because it appeals to you, but because you love him more than what naturally delights you! Boy, who ever said parenting was easy? Remember, God never calls us to do something at the expense of our children.

A Clean House. Cleanliness and orderliness is a godly character quality we need to aim for and train our children in, but it's never more important than our children's spirits. I want a clean, orderly house for my family to live in, but I also want them to have freedom to live and grow and experiment and play.

You've heard it said, "Where no oxen are, the manger is clean"? We shouldn't make our children so paranoid of making a mess that they never have freedom to explore, to dream, to invent. Our house is not to be a showpiece but a greenhouse. As much as possible, try to create a place for everything, but relax when everything may not be in its place but learning is happening.

What I've done often with the little ones is have several pick-up times during the day: before school in the morning, again before naptime, before supper and before bedtime. If it's not clear as to who is responsible for what (Tim took it out, Kate, Matt and Emmy played with it), then I assign a room to each child or two children, and they work until it's cleaned up. You don't have to have a House Beautiful every day.

The fact that company is coming is not sufficient reason to get upset with all the children, hollering orders to try to get everything picture perfect. Company is probably not even going to notice the dust on the shelf anyway. Pick up the clutter, vacuum the floor and be ready to enjoy your company instead of stressing everyone so much that they dread hearing "company's coming!"

The impression you make on others. God made you the way you are and each one of your family the way they are. Be yourself, let the kids be themselves, train them in advance for how you expect them to act, but don't worry about fitting into some imaginary perfect mold or someone else's expectations. Lighten up, train your children to serve God together with Mom and Dad, and leave the rest to God to work out. Most important is the impression we leave stamped on our children's hearts.

Our convenience and comfort. Newsflash – children weren't entrusted to us for our convenience. They are God's treasures, entrusted to our care for a limited time only. God will hold us accountable for how we invested our time in those treasures. We think when our children are babies that we have forever to train them, but that time flies by and is never regained. You can't get back wasted time. Children will grow and leave home, and if you haven't made them a priority, all the good intentions in the world don't count. So, get off the couch, go out to the sandbox, and build that castle. There's no better time than today.

Our pleasure. Pleasure and entertainment, I believe, are idols in today's society. Anything that displaces God's preeminence in our life is an idol. Our culture is saturated with this line of thought: "You deserve a break today," "You owe it to yourself". We see it on billboards, hear it on TV, hear it on the radio, in magazines, and from people all around us. People rush home on Fridays to "have a good weekend", which often means indulging in our own pleasures, whatever they may be. I believe God created us to benefit from recreation, but our society has pushed God to the back burner and embraced pleasure in His place. Let us beware and not make the mistake of leading our children on that path. Don't neglect your children while you spend your time on your own pleasures.

Our time. Time is our most precious commodity. How we spend our time is how we spend our life. Do our kids know, beyond the shadow of a doubt, that we love them enough to give them our time? It's a balancing act, I must admit, especially when you have a large family. At times, I feel like a rubber band stretched out in multiple directions, but ultimately, my kids know my heart. Even if each one can't get my time exactly the instant they want it, they know they're a priority and I'm more concerned about them even if I'm giving time to another person right now – I'll get to them and I *want* to get to them.

It takes constant evaluation to make sure you're not committed in too many other areas. Schedules change, kids' ages change, and I need to be certain I'm spending my time wisely. God also gives promptings, like, "Hey, Kelley needs special time. Drop something you're doing and give her time, or take her along when you do errands."

Do a heart check. Is your heart first committed to God? Are you then yielded to Him in the area of letting His love flow through you to your children? Do they know they have your heart? If so, you'll have theirs. It's a natural response. If you don't have their heart, do some inspection – look at your heart and ask God to reveal blind spots to you. He will. After all, you're doing this for Him!

Our first child! Son Rick was born on my birthday, screaming and kicking. He hasn't slowed down since!

We started homeschooling about this time, when we had four children. From left: Rick, Nate, Tim, baby Josh and our Irish Setter Bonnie.

Finally, a girl! Katie, our fifth child, was adored by her older brothers, who played with her constantly.

For Matthew, our sixth child, anatomy was his favorite subject. Here he is, hard at work.

Katie's training for beauty school. The young cosmetologist!

Tim, Carrie, Matt and Emily (with blankie!) help Josh (center) celebrate his birthday. Happy Birthday, Josh!

Here's little Matt, in front of our neighbors' Christmas tree farm. We got our trees here for years.

Emmy, Matt, Kate, Carrie and Christa in chairs their dad made out of buckets from his job. Creative, and cheap, too!

Matt and Emmy were special buddies at this age. It looks like Carrie's blazing her own trail!

Emmy is "helping" Mommy take care of little sister Laura.

Tuck (with pacifier firmly in place) joins sisters Laura and Grace at play in the kitchen.

Emmy takes her turn with Baby Grace. The swing was a favorite spot for all the babies.

Tuck was Josh's little buddy. They were especially close during Josh's fight with leukemia.

Mommy Laura "reads" Bible stories to her doll family.

Carrie's enjoying her 5th birthday party! Birthdays were one time to eat junk food without having to sneak it!

Rick and Christina married in 2001. They now have a son, Luke Douglas. They did the graphic design for my book, and hope to start a design business.

Nate and Tina married in 2000. We welcomed our first daughter-in-law to the family.

From left to right, Nate, Tim, and Rick, on a sunny day at the Peaks of Otter in Virginia. Their sizes show who's oldest.

Tim and Kari wed in 2003. They now have a beautiful daughter, Cassidy Lynn.

From left to right, Nate, Tim, and Rick, at the same location. Now who's the biggest?

Kelley and Kasey, our two youngest girls, scout the Wild West (actually our dining room) for robbers and crooks.

Kelley is proud of her artwork! She still loves getting into messes.

Brittany is the family's animal lover. She's here with Rick's bloodhound, Sadie. Brittany spends time each day training the family's pets.

Tuck and Kelley were ringbearer and flower girl for Rick and Christina's wedding. Tuck wowed all the ladies. How CUTE!!

Tuck and Nate are special buddies. They like to go hunting together, and sometimes Nate and his wife Tina will invite Tuck to spend the night with them.

We won!!! Our son Rick was elected to local office in 2003. He introduced his family as "the best campaign team in Campbell County."

Rick gives his victory speech on election night. He defeated a two-term incumbent by 15 points.

Our youngest, Kasey, campaigns for her big brother at his press conference announcing his bid for office.

Kasey plays on the deck in our backyard. She is always dreaming up games and is quite the little actor.

Here's me and son Rick in 2004. I can't believe it's been 30 years!

Tuck, our youngest boy, celebrates his birthday during our family vacation at the beach. Sister Kasey asks, "When will it be my birthday?"

Kasey (left) and Kelley enjoy the sunset at the beach. They love to play in the water and look for seashells.

Nate's wife Tina (left) and Kate at the beach. They'd just eaten at a seafood restaurant with other family members.

From left: Tuck, Laura, Kasey, Kelley, and Brittany. We took this picture in Fall 2003 on the day we bought pumpkins to decorate our home. Pumpkin picking is an annual tradition in our family.

Our family at the beach. We rented a house on the shore, and our children who've moved out came along, too. Our children like our vacations together so much, they start planning the next year's as soon as they get home.

Our first grandchild, Cassidy Lynn, arrived July 17, 2004. Some of our own babies were born in the same hospital room!

Kasey, our youngest, holds grandson Luke. Kasey was especially taken with him. "He's just the right size for me!"

Rick and I have shared a lot of years together. We've been through joyous times and scary times, but we've always faced them together.

Carrie, our third daughter, loves babies. She sits here with Cassidy Lynn.

Proud parents Tim and Kari welcomed baby Cassidy in July 2004. I'm a grandma!

 Chapter Sixteen

We Have This Moment, Today

I remember so clearly one warm sunny day in May. I had seven children at the time, one just two weeks old. The kids were outside playing under the sprinkler, laughing, making up games. God spoke so clearly to my heart that day, saying, "Cherish this day. Bask in this moment." I did, and I still do now. Today, three of those little boys are married, two have children of their own, and one of the boys is in heaven, which makes that memory even more precious to me. A dear friend of ours, Doug Oldham, sang a song that I have treasured through the years. It goes like this:

**"We have this moment to hold in our hands,
And to touch as it slips through our fingers like sand.
Yesterday's gone, and tomorrow may never come,
But we have this moment today."**

My prayer is that God will burn that truth in each of your hearts and cause you to "number your days, that you may apply your hearts unto wisdom" (Psalm 90:12). Time is not forever. As a young mom, I thought the season of life I was experiencing (an infant, a couple of toddlers, a preschooler, dirty diapers, in-depth training) would last forever. It seemed impossible to imagine anything different. And yes, looking back, it now seems like each season only lasted a short time and I find myself wishing that season back again, even for just one day!

Each season has blessings all its own. Yes, it has its own struggles and challenges, but focus on the blessings. For instance, it was definitely more difficult to manage when I had three little ones and all the laundry, chores, meals, etc., to do by myself. Yet now I look back on those days as peaceful and sweet in their own way. The little boys all took naps and I had a time of peace and quiet in the afternoon. I set the schedule and actually had control over it. Bedtime was easy. Now, there's always so much going on that it's hard for little ones to sleep.

Rick and I always used to have some quiet evening time to talk and plan. Now we have to do that when we go out to eat. Our house is always a busy place, people coming and going, and when you pull in the driveway, you never know who'll be there. And yet, my girls fix meals, the kids do the chores, so things are easier now on that score. I have plenty of babysitters so I don't have to take four little ones with me when I run errands.

I'm not saying one season is better than another, but that each has its blessings. If we learn to focus on its blessings and not its irritations, we can learn to cooperate with it. Instead of resisting it, embrace it, throw yourself into it. Young mom, don't feel guilty for not being involved in a lot of church functions and leadership roles. Maximize your time as a young mom. There's nothing more important you can be doing with your time than investing it in your little ones and leading them to God.

You see, God plans our "life curriculum," and, as with our children, things work best when we cooperate with His plan. Some seasons are a huge struggle. It's hard to be pregnant, feeling sick, and still responsible to train other children, but God gives grace. Look for the positives. When you're feeling really sick, let the older kids have the opportunity to practice their cooking skills and parenting skills sometimes, too. After Laura was born, Rick and Tim fixed me cream of wheat every day for a month. It was great. They developed leadership skills and I found that cream of wheat isn't so bad every morning, especially when you don't have to cook it yourself!

I also learned through eleven years of pregnancy that when you're not feeling well, it's usually better for the morale for you to be up and functioning as best you can instead of focusing on how rotten you feel. I figure God uses all that to build strong bonds between our hearts and the children's. We suffered much to bring them into the world, and where our treasure is, there will our heart be also.

God is the grace supplier. We can't do it on our own. He doesn't want us to. He wants us to be aware of our total dependence on Him. When God brings about circumstances beyond our control, turn to Him for strength.

We had a very trying time back in 1999, when my Dad was struggling with cancer. He lived in Massachusetts, and we're in Virginia. For almost a three-month period, he suffered much as the doctors tried to figure out what was wrong. I tried to be there as much as I could to help him and give my older sister a break, also. Kasey was just nine months old at the time, so I usually took a babysitter/helper, often Matt, to help me navigate the 13-hour trip. It's never been easy to leave my family, but Dad needed help, and it just wasn't an option not to go. As time went on, my older sons would help by going up to stay for a week at a time so I could be home sometimes too.

It was an extremely rough period, but I am so thankful that we all pitched in to help my Dad in his time of need. It was the right thing to do and Dad appreciated it, and God taught us all lessons of what really counts in life. It was one of those rough times that you'd never want to do over again, but wouldn't trade for anything, either. To confirm to my Dad that we cared about him is worth all the inconvenient hardship many times over.

We have this moment to hold in our hands – some of those moments are wonderful, precious memories. We take lots of pictures. We have lots of occasions – birthdays, special nights out, Bible verse lunches out, fun plan and fix a meal nights, fun trips, Bible quiz nights, picnics, cookouts, special Sunday night supper get-togethers. Life is precious and God has blessed us so abundantly. Try to give your children some encouragement and motivation along the way, for all these things build good memories.

The girls and I love to scrapbook and talk over all the details of past events as we journal about them. Family is important. Make it fun to belong to your family. A little laughter goes a long way. When Nate was little, he wrote,

We have this moment, today

"A merry heart does good like a medicine", illustrated the verse, and we hung it in our house for years. We laugh a lot! It's good medicine for the soul. We've had some guests leave saying their cheeks hurt from laughing so much.

Make the most of your moments today. Loosen up, look for the positive in whatever you're going through, and make the memories you'll all be able to sit around and laugh about for years to come!

 Chapter Seventeen

From Sorrow To Joy

It was about 11:15 on a warm sunny September morning when my telephone rang. It was Gene from the doctor's office. He asked me if Rick was home and I said no, he was at work. He told me he had some bad news and perhaps I should sit down. I told him I was sitting, and he proceeded to tell me that Josh's test results had come back, and although he wasn't positive, it appeared that Josh had leukemia.

At that very moment, my life changed drastically, although I couldn't comprehend how much just then. I was stunned. I don't remember too much else that he said, except that I should get in touch with Rick and have him call Gene. He would schedule us with an oncologist that afternoon to confirm the diagnosis.

Rick, my husband, was a drywall contractor. My third oldest son, Nate, worked for him. I knew they were supposed to be at a house near to home today. I got in the car and drove there, feeling as if nothing was quite real. Nate was there by himself. Rick was wrapping up another job and was due to arrive soon. I told Nate, eighteen years old, that Josh, his younger brother by eighteen months, had leukemia they thought, and told him I needed to reach Dad. He asked me if I was okay and offered to call Dad on his cell phone for me. He did, told him the news, and heard him say, "yes, Mom seems to be okay." Rick was on his way home. Nate offered to stay on the job and keep the work going.

I rode home. I remember sitting on the couch wondering how I could tell Josh. Should I tell Josh? What was leukemia anyway? I'd heard of it, but I couldn't explain it – my impressions were vague. I called the church to notify them. I did okay until I said the word 'leukemia', and broke into tears, but was able to calm myself as I asked Jean to tell the pastors.

Josh called me. "Maw, come here." He was lying on his bed, with a very bad headache and he was extremely weak. He'd been to the doctor on Friday, and they suspected he had mono. The symptoms were very much the same.

Josh had been having headaches for a few months. He'd been to the doctor twice, and had been on antibiotics for a suspected sinus infection. The first round of antibiotic had no effect, so they tried a stronger one. Still no effect. Just lately, he'd gotten short of breath when he expended energy. He'd even thrown up a couple of times.

He had been helping some good friends roof their house that summer, and had to get off the roof to throw up. When he mowed grass (he worked for a landscaping company), he'd have to rest often.

The previous Friday, September 6th, we had had the

strong effects of a hurricane. Water began to seep into our finished basement. The boys and Rick were vacuuming it out, but the water had the upper hand and it was all they could do to keep up with it. Josh was down there helping, but he was very weak. He volunteered to go to Lowes for the third vacuum. I was eight and a half months pregnant so I wasn't much help in the basement. Josh took a little longer than expected to get the vacuum. He was moving slower than usual. He took it downstairs and started helping the group.

A while later he came up and sat down in the recliner and said, "Maw, I feel so guilty. They need my help, but I'm all worn out. I just can't do it anymore. My head is killing me and I'm so short of breath. I think I really need to go to the doctor again. This medicine just isn't helping at all."

I was pretty overwhelmed to say the least. Everything in the basement needed to be put up high. The water was coming in faster than three guys could vacuum it. I called the doctor and they said for him to come on in. Josh said, "Mom, you stay here. I'll drive myself." I agreed. Off he went, while I set about supervising the overwhelming job in the basement. The rain finally let up. There was lots of water to be vacuumed up, but it finally quit flowing in. What a job lay ahead of us!

Josh came back home a couple of hours later. He was pretty upset; he had hit a border collie who had run out in front of his truck, and he couldn't stop quick enough. A farmer had come out as the dog was in pain and howling. The farmer told him it was a stray – chased cars and was bound to be hit. He'd take care of it for Josh. Josh loved dogs. Collies were his favorite, and he felt really bad.

He said Gene had told him that he suspected a bad case of mono. He took a blood test, and the results would be back Monday morning. Josh must stay really quiet in bed most of the weekend, as his spleen was enlarged and Gene didn't want to risk it rupturing. Josh didn't object. He didn't feel up to anything but heading off to bed. The dog too, was still heavy on his mind. Josh slept a lot that weekend. He didn't have much of an appetite – he was a pretty sick boy.

He was calling me into his room. He said, "Maw, what do I have?" I said, "Well, Gene's not positive." "Maw, tell me." What could I say? I just said, "Well, he thinks you've got leukemia. We have to go to another doctor this afternoon to make sure." With relief in his voice, he said, "Oh. I knew it was bad by the look on your face. I'm sure glad it wasn't AIDS or something."

Rick arrived and we waited for the oncologist to call. We didn't have to wait too long; we were able to go in at 1:30. Josh walked slowly into the office. He was really weak. The office was full of pale, mostly elderly people. The doctors drew blood, examined it under microscopes and confirmed that it was leukemia. We were to take Josh to the University of Virginia Medical Center as soon as we could be ready to leave.

We went home and gathered up a few of his things in a suitcase. Pastor Brodie, the assistant pastor at our church, was waiting for us at home. Josh sunk into the recliner and called Tucker, his two year old brother, up onto his lap. They were best buddies. Josh loved Tuck dearly and took him lots of places in his new truck. Josh had been working for a landscaper since March, and had saved his money to buy his much-wanted truck. It was his prized possession – a 1982 Ford F100 – garage kept, excellent condition.

Although his head was pounding, he held Tuck and told him he had to go to the hospital for a few days, and asked Tuck if he'd watch his truck for him. As Rick drove off to UVA, Tuck waved furiously and then climbed on the bumper of Josh's truck, held on, and stood there "watching" it for him, as he would do often in the next weeks in Josh's absence.

We found out that the headaches were caused by massive amounts of white blood cells in his bloodstream. The normal range is 10-12,000. Josh's white blood count was over two hundred thousand, up considerably even since the previous Friday when blood was drawn. That night they administered a blood feresis - taking his blood out of one arm, straining it of white cells and putting it back into the other arm. Josh was so sick he just didn't care much, although he always hated needles, and the ones they used for this procedure were large. They had to repeat this process the following night also to get those white cells down.

The headaches were better. Now began some of the most trying and mind-blowing times in my life. We had long meetings with doctors; they being familiar with medical terms and procedures explaining to us the risks, the tests, the prognosis, the possible complications. The fact that Josh would probably never be able to have children due to high doses of chemotherapy and later radiation was a hard pill for me to swallow. Josh loved little kids. Tuck was the delight of his life.

As I look back, the things that scared me so much were small in comparison to the fact that his very life was at stake, but I hadn't comprehended that yet. Josh begged us to sign for them to put in a Heinlich catheter, so they could administer medicines without needles. But a central line into your bloodstream so close to your heart seemed so invasive to us. We assented. It was the first of many signatures which so often felt like I was signing my son's life away.

It was suggested we switch Josh to pediatrics. He was seventeen, and borderline between child and adult age. We made the decision to do so, and were so glad we did. We were assigned a social worker, as were all patients. That really made us apprehensive at first. After all, we were home educators and fourteen years earlier had had to defend our stand in court. "Social worker" were two words we didn't want to hear. But upon meeting her, we found she was hand-picked by God. Her sister had seven kids and home educated them. Her sister later wrote us a letter thanking us for Josh's influence on her sister's life, and saying that God had hand-picked us to help reach Teresa. She was Catholic and her sister said that God kept putting Christian witnesses in her path.

We soon found out that there are hundreds of kinds of leukemia. Josh had AML, a very aggressive, fast moving blood cancer. Then we learned that there are various types of AML. Of course we always hoped his would be easy to cure. It was number seven on a scale of one to ten, ten being the worst.

We underwent numerous briefings by his main doctor, whom we liked very much. It was mind-boggling. They had to tell you all the possible complications and we had to sign that we understood that any of these might eventually happen. All the time we hung on to the positive things. He was first given a seventy percent chance of survival. We hung on. We listened. We asked questions. We asked more questions. We just knew it would be okay.

Josh was involved with all the decisions. I felt that was only right. He never wanted anything held back from him, although he didn't care to hear all the what-ifs that we had to hear. He said he'd deal with things as they happened. He told his dad the first night when he asked Josh if he was scared, "The word 'scared' is not in my vocabulary." His faith in God was immovable. His focus was on others.

Josh's treatment plan was a week-long course of strong chemotherapy, followed by a five-day chemo intended to put him into remission. Then, as soon as his white blood count would surface again and they were sure he was in remission, a bone marrow transplant would be scheduled. Josh's leukemia was rare and aggressive - a one in one-hundred- thousand chance of getting that type of AML.

The treatment was also aggressive. The briefings about chemo and its complications as well as the bone marrow transplant...overwhelming is not a strong enough word to describe them. The human brain not trained in medicine was on overload to try to absorb all that was scheduled to take place. Chemo was begun immediately.

Josh was very nauseated. They tried for several days to combat nausea. We found he was allergic to Phenegrin and had an allergic reaction, a shaking, squirming feeling in his skin, much worse than the nausea itself. Finally they tried ATIVAN. It worked best for him. He always had nausea to a degree, but that was what controlled it best of all. It made him sleepy, but he said he'd rather sleep than feel sick. It did lower his heart rate significantly, and scared the doctors several times, so they had to monitor him carefully. We learned that chemo takes a while to work, and blood counts continue to plummet after the treatment is over. His counts would have to come up some before he could come home.

At first, my days were spent with OB visits (they monitored this pregnancy carefully, considering the extra stress) at 7 am, a fifty-minute ride home, packing up to go to UVA, another hour and a half drive, staying until 10 or 11 at night, and back home to grab a bite of supper and go to bed. Kelley was born in between Josh's first and second rounds of chemo, while he was home, thankfully. I came home the next day, and the following week Josh had to go up for round number two. This one was five days long, and as the hospital was one and a half hours away, I stayed home and talked long hours with Josh on the phone. Rick went up to be with him each day.

By the third round of chemo, I just took Kelley with me each day and often we spent the night up there in Josh's room. There were several weeks that Josh had complications and couldn't come home. He loved it when I would spend the nights with him. He had trouble sleeping

during the nights, so he appreciated the company. He did have several periods at home, always with a packed suitcase, ready at a moment's notice to head back to UVA should he spike a fever. During home times, we still had two days a week that we'd go up to the clinic for the day for blood and platelet tests, etc.

The goal was to get Josh into remission and then give him a bone marrow transplant. Matt, thirteen, was a perfect match to Josh. At one point, the local newspaper came to interview Josh. Josh gave a clear testimony and told them he was in a win-win situation. Either he'd be healed here on earth, or in heaven. Josh struggled with not having energy to do things he wanted to do, but his spirit was strong. He believed what I'd told him from the time he was little, that God made Him in a special way for a special purpose.

He got a fever after the reporter left, and had to be rushed to UVA again. That night he told me, "Maw, I really think God held that fever back 'til I finished that interview."

God did use the interview. The paper actually printed his clear gospel message and Josh got a lot of response. An eighty year old man wrote to him, who said he'd never written a letter in his life, but told him he was touched by his testimony.

Josh never achieved a full remission. We came within one day of the beginning of transplant when leukemia showed up again. We even tried an experimental chemo, but nothing worked. I remember the day the doctor came in to tell Josh that the experimental chemotherapy hadn't worked, and there was nothing left to try. Josh looked at him and said, "Dr. DeAlercon, it must be really hard for you to have to give people such bad news." The doctor's eyes teared up and he was very affected by Josh, he told us later.

Josh came home, where he wanted to be, still hoping to regain enough strength to go through with the transplant, even if he wasn't in remission. He hoped to gain a little more time to live, but strength didn't return, and he got weaker.

He was always my right-hand man. Rick had apprenticed the other boys in drywall, but Josh had been my helper. We had done all my many errands together. He helped me shop for good buys, keeping in his head what was a better deal at which store. He was my good friend. I knew him so well and he knew me. He had my heart, and I had his.

The night before he died, I remember he asked Nate, his brother, to help him to his swollen feet. Nate asked why, and he said, "I need to go help Mom. She needs me." That was his heart. He was my helper.

He died at home where he wanted to be, just after Rick had finished reading John 14 to him.

During the time he was sick, we heard from people in every state and 18 foreign countries who were praying for him. There were 24-hour prayer chains going for Josh. I have no doubt that God could have healed him, as people were praying, but God had other plans for Josh.

Shortly after he died, I felt that if Josh could have talked to me, he would have said, "Maw, it's okay. I understand now, and I'll explain it to you when you get here." I asked God to show me a little part of why He chose to take Josh home, and God has, in His mercy, poured out myriads of reasons. I have a real peace that I did my best with Josh, he did his best for his Lord, and God has received much glory.

We counted 18 people who had asked Jesus in their heart during the time Josh was sick and immediately following. At his memorial service, a friend of our family, just a few years older than Josh, was there and God convicted her as others shared testimonies about Josh. She said God asked her, "What would others say about you if you were to die right now?" She was involved in drinking, smoking, bad music, etc., and God used that to turn her around and get her and her husband excited about serving Him.

We heard testimonies of husbands and wives who started praying with each other for the first time, family devotions starting up and becoming regular, as they prayed faithfully for Josh. One of Josh's best friends testified that Josh's testimony through his time of illness turned his life around. He was started down the wrong path, but God used the whole experience to cause him to dedicate his life over again, and now he is serving God as a pastor.

Each year since that time, we've been involved in a benefit concert to help another child with leukemia. We have the opportunity to minister to the family in ways that others can't who haven't been through it and know the roller coaster ride of emotion you go through. Every year at the concert, an invitation is given and people are saved. Tuck, Josh's little buddy, was saved at one of the benefit concerts; little Kasey, our youngest, who never got to meet Josh, was saved at another.

Our dear friend Doug Phillips gave us the honor of attending Josh's memorial service, and he says that it was a life-changing event for him, one that he shares with thousands of people around the country. Gene, the nurse practitioner who diagnosed Josh (the first child he'd ever diagnosed with cancer), attended the service and also told us it changed him for life and helped him to be able to better counsel his patients who lose a child.

We've received letters from hundreds of parents who prayed for Josh, telling how the experience affected their family for eternity. Every few months, God blesses me with another testimony we hadn't known about. God is so good.

I remember the verse I was meditating on at the time Josh got sick – Philippians 4:7, about the peace of God. I was feeling a bit overwhelmed with all my responsibilities as mom and wife, and was earnestly praying for peace. One day on my way to Charlottesville, after having left my other kids at home, I remember crying out to God and telling Him this wasn't what I meant when I was praying for peace. I was praying for circumstantial peace, but God was answering my prayer for true peace.

I didn't understand it then, but I do now. I do have real peace. I did my job with Josh. I have no regrets. He did his job for God, and God in His sovereignty has used it and blessed and impacted multitudes of lives, and I only know a small part of how He used the whole thing to glorify Himself and bring others into His kingdom and gain victory in their pilgrimages.

It may be that some of you reading this book will have to release a child to heaven. You expect to lose your parents, but not your child. Should it happen, God's grace must be appropriated. He won't force it on you, but it's there for the asking. It's not a judgment on you; on the contrary, God wants to use it mightily, and if you'll cooperate with Him, He'll do just that. There's a song that addresses this so well:

"God is too wise to be mistaken.
God is too good to be unkind.
So when you don't understand,
When you don't see His plan,
When you can't trace His hand,
Trust His heart."

It was a consuming desire of mine that Josh's suffering not be wasted. God doesn't make mistakes. I feel God chose to use Josh to accomplish much for eternity, and that's a privilege. Our children aren't really our own. They're His.

Heaven has taken on a whole new dimension for me. I used to think, sure, someday! But now I view it with anticipation. I can't wait to get to heaven and see the finished side of God's tapestry. We'll find out how other people down through the ages influenced us and how we influenced others, and how things we couldn't make sense of down here on earth were weaved into a masterpiece in heaven! It's exciting! And heaven lasts forever! Our time on earth is so brief. In heaven we'll enjoy eternity, together, and that's *forever!*

Chapter Eighteen

Blessings of Many

We've been asked if we're Catholic, if we're Mormon, if we're crazy. Yes, we know what causes it and no, we shouldn't get a TV.

We got married, like everyone else, assuming birth control was just what you were 'supposed to do'. It was when Rick was attending a college family life class that we arrived on our decision to place our trust in the Creator of the universe in this matter. The professor was listing all the reasons why you should use birth control, and it struck Rick that all his reasons were extremely selfish ones. It was this that inspired Rick to study children in scripture and see what God had to say.

It was incredible! Children are always a blessing, a gift in scripture. When God wanted to bless someone, He sent them a child. (See appendix #6 for a listing of scriptures we found; also, we highly recommend Rick and Jan Hess' book "A Full Quiver". Rick and Jan give a great presentation and I like the section in the back that answers all the questions you generally hear in support of birth control).

In a nutshell, God, the creator of the universe, is omniscient and knows much better than we do how many children we ought to have. After all, He has a master plan and our children fit into it.

Often when I would find out I was expecting, I'd think, oh boy, why now? But God always knew even when I didn't. For instance, Kelley was born three weeks after Josh was diagnosed with leukemia, and it was anything but easy being pregnant with all those trips to UVA and then having to bring little Kelley, her playpen and diapers and clothes, etc., to 'live' with Josh at UVA. But God knew. Josh loved kids and it was a joy to him to have Kelley and Tuck around, even when he felt lousy. It helped to bring part of home to him in his hospital room, so God knew!

I could recount situations where finances were looking rough when a baby came, but in every instance, God knew, and He makes no mistakes. Looking back, I wouldn't have fewer children. Rick and I are not rich in earthly goods but in posterity – true riches.

I can unequivocally say, without hesitation, that one of my biggest joys in life is to watch my older kids interact with the younger ones. I love it! Nate will call Tuck and take him fishing or hunting or to spend the night at his house; Tim comes to take the younger kids to the farm he rents to play with the animals or repair fences. The younger kids look forward to the others coming home. Matt takes some of the little ones with him to help take trash to the dump and often buy them a treat at the store.

My kids are each others' best friends. The married kids and the older ones who still live at home generally get together each weekend at one of the houses and eat together and fellowship. We've just finished helping Tim and Kari fix up the house they just bought – patch walls, paint, strip wallpaper, freshen up.

When Rick was campaigning for his supervisor race, we all were knocking on doors, passing out literature, making phone calls. Last spring we needed to paint the trim on our house, so I called a painting party. All the older kids came over and we did it all in one Saturday. Then we had a cookout as we sat back and enjoyed a job quickly done.

We draw names at Christmas time and each one buys gifts for three other people. It's so fun watching everyone plan surprises for each other. I've made ceramic nativity sets for each of my married kids, as everyone loves the one I made back in 1977.

On Thanksgiving, Kari and Kate started a tradition of a Thanksgiving wreath, decorated with miniatures representing major events or accomplishments in each person's life during the past year. We also do a 'time capsule' and put a paper with questions to fill out such as blessings, significant events, goals and spiritual accomplishments in the past year.

There is almost always a celebration at our house. With Mom, Dad, thirteen kids, three daughters-in-law and a grandchild, there is always a party.

Everyone gets to choose their birthday supper and what sort of celebration they want – climbing Peaks of Otter and a picnic, renting a boat on Smith Mountain Lake for the day, a cookout, inviting friends over, dinner at a restaurant, etc. It's always something different and something fun.

Life is ever so busy, but ever so fulfilling. My kids have learned and are learning how to get along with multiple personality types – we've got 'em all, and our family is growing.

Every Sunday night after church, we have all the kids over to the house for supper, along with various friends they invite. We usually don't know exactly who we'll have until we get there. We prepare lots of food, but when it's gone, it's gone. Sometimes after supper, the kids will sing around the piano.

Rick and I, at this stage in our lives, go out to eat often, just to talk. It's not ever easy to carry on a conversation, even if everyone is being good! We often comment that we wonder who'll be there when we get home.

Yes, a large family is a lot of work, takes lots of commitment, and costs a lot of money. If we hadn't had fourteen kids, we'd have a lot of money, but I'd honestly rather have the kids. The joy of investing your life in children and watching them grow up to serve God is worth so much more than money can buy. It's eternal investment, unlike houses and land. I believe God is raising up a multitude of large families who are raising a godly generation who will pass on the torch to their children.

Let me clarify, though, that I believe God is sovereign. I don't think everyone should have a large family. I believe God has a different plan for each person, and if He doesn't give you a large family, rejoice in the special opportunity to invest extra time in the one or two kids you have. It could just be that your child has a special mission

and he or she needs extra input and a closer relationship
with you than would be possible if you had more children.
God knows! Trust Him!

 Chapter Nineteen

Train Him in His Own Way

We've found that each one of our children is different from the next. Some things are universal and all children must be taught such truths. For instance, all children should learn the Ten Commandments, scripture memorization, character qualities, Bible stories, and then time alone with God. God's truth and principles are for everyone.

God is the master of creativity and He does His finest work in people. We are each created in God's image, but at the same time, we are a unique combination of different personality types, possessing different amounts of natural talents and abilities, motivating gifts, etc. God is so creative that no two people are just alike.

It's a natural tendency of man to assume that everyone else thinks and reacts and responds just like we do. We tend to see others from our point of view only. We need to learn to, as scripture says, "be all things to all people." We need to learn to look at life from their point of view instead of trying to force everyone into our mold. It's so important that we understand this with our children.

I remember clearly one occasion when one of our boys was very small. He was embarrassed about something, but he always showed that embarrassment with what appeared to be anger. I remember calling Rick aside and pointing that out to him, as he was about to punish the child for an angry spirit. Being the mom, I'd seen it happen before, and Rick agreed when I called his attention to it. This child seemed to have a tough exterior, but really had a soft, sensitive heart underneath.

Rick and I thought we had parenting down pat when our oldest was about eighteen months old, and then Tim was born. Rick and Tim were and still are vastly different from each other. It kept happening, every eighteen months to two years, and each one was different from the others. Rules are the same, principles are the same, truth is the same, but how you deal with each child's spirit varies. It's a matter of heart. The parents' heart cries out to God's heart to learn how to minister and nurture each child's heart.

The differences manifest themselves in so many ways. For instance, one of my boys would build up a mental block whenever I'd show him a new concept, especially in math. His immediate and consistent response to a new math concept would be, "Oh no, I can't do it. It's too hard. I'll never understand it." I'd have to gently show him how to work the problems by doing them myself and then helping him do a few, and all of a sudden, he'd respond with, "Oh, that was easy!" But next new concept, the initial reaction was the same.

Another son would fight with being grumpy while doing school. Hands-on was his thing. Books were not a consuming love, as they were for his older brother. He'd rather be off tinkering with something – fixing, building, creating. So his natural reaction was to be grumpy at the start of school time. I finally realized that he just needed to lighten up. I'd often just play with him a bit, tickle him, laugh about something, and he'd be okay and settle down to get his work done so he could be off to his own pursuits.

Another of my children did the best to do her least. In other words, I had to check up on her, stay on top of what she was (or more likely wasn't) doing, and make use of tests more often than I did with the other kids.

Others were more self-directed and could be trusted to set goals, accomplish self-imposed deadlines, and pace themselves. Some were not confident in some subjects and needed to be kept behind long enough to gain confidence that they could do it, and then leap ahead.

One taught himself to read at age five. Another was extremely slow to catch on to reading, having a strong science/math brain and being painfully frustrated at the inconsistency of the English language. Put in his own words, "Mom, the person who wrote the English language had a pencil in one hand and a jug in the other!" The constant breaking of its own rules really upset him, but in his time, slow and steady, it clicked, and he just recently told me, "Mom, I figure now I can read just for fun!" Wow! I had begun to wonder if he'd ever read fluently. In the meantime though, he had an advanced vocabulary and loved to listen to G.A. Henty books on tape. In so doing, he was acquiring a wonderful knowledge of all sorts of time periods of history and was very comfortable with the old English way of speaking.

The temptation to try to have all your children follow the schedule the last one did won't usually work that way. Don't compare one child to another. God gives each his own strengths, and that's part of God's plan for each child. Teach your children to appreciate each other's strengths, as being given by God.

A book we've found very helpful is "Five Love Languages of Children." Also, studying about spiritual gifts is very helpful. "The Treasure Tree" is another book by Gary Smalley, written for children, that helps them discern the four basic personality types and appreciate how God uses each one to complement the other.

Our son Rick, who does drywall himself, has often said that Tim is the best drywall man in town. Rick, on the other hand, is gifted with boldness and a strong sense of justice, which has enabled him to withstand tremendous pressure in the political arena. I understand now exactly why God gave Rick the temperament and gift of prophecy that He did. Rick would stand up to the very gates of Hell to defend righteousness and truth when I would be looking for a bed to hide under.

Tim, on the other hand, is a perfectionist, very skilled and excellent in handiwork, and is an excellent musician and singer. Precision and excellence are paramount for him. Nate, our third son, is a master in peacemaking. He has a special gift to see life from another person's point of view and bring peace about in sticky situations.

Those natural tendencies and strong character traits that your children seem to be born with are just that. We all can be trained to grow in character, but the gifts that God gives each one of us are specially imparted to each person to help them fulfill his mission for their lives. We're supposed to be different, and each one can learn from other's strengths. Let's cooperate with God's plan instead of competing with it!

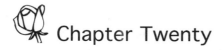 Chapter Twenty

Beware Of Bitterness

I believe Satan hates families, especially families who are training their children to serve God. I believe Satan's biggest tool to destroy family harmony is bitterness. Hebrews 12:15 says, "See to it that no root of bitterness, springing up, causes trouble and by it many be defiled."

Bitterness is a subtle thing. Satan knows he can't get the average Christian to forsake the faith and follow him, so he settles for a sneak attack, hoping to hinder our usefulness (I Pet. 5:8, "Be sober, be vigilant, because your adversary the devil, as a roaring lion, walketh about, seeking whom he may devour").

I have a strong burden for Christian families. Harboring bitterness is never worth it. Bitterness always brings about death to relationships. As home educators, we need to doubly guard against this. We are investing our time, energies, schedule - in short, our lives - into the lives of our children. I think there's a strong tendency to become bitter when we feel like we've invested so much and our kids don't appreciate it, or haven't done what we expected them to do. In some ways, we have added pressure from others to see that our kids 'conform' to expectations of excellence, academic proficiency, etc. We are tempted to put pressure on our kids to conform to what others think they should be doing. We must guard against this and let God lead each child as He sees fit, not what others pressure us to do.

Parents, we must set the godly example. A clue that you may be harboring bitterness is feeling hurt often. Bitterness masquerades as hurt, which is actually selfishness. Another symptom is that a bitter person is hardly ever able to be pleased. It's almost like he has a chip on his shoulder and walks about looking to be offended. He gets offended very easily. When offended, he dredges up all the past offenses toward him and dwells on them. He hasn't turned whatever it is over to God, but hangs on to it himself and it colors his eyeglasses, so to speak.

A bitter person is not always exhibiting bitterness. Sometimes it's masked, but springs up to cause trouble when he is irritated. He has a tendency to expect the worst in the person he is harboring bitterness toward. The offender's faults overshadow their positive qualities in his eyes and he tends to live with a defeated spirit.

If you sense any of these characteristics in your life or your loved ones, examine yourself for bitterness and relinquish it. Don't destroy the very thing you've been working for all these years by allowing bitterness to dwell within. Learn not to take things personally, but give hurts and disappointments to God. We must realize that bitterness seems to be directed at people, but it is ultimately toward God. Confess it to God and give no place to the devil!

God allows trials to come into our lives to make us *better*. Satan fights to get us to become *bitter*. We as parents must, first of all, realize that our kids probably won't appreciate all you've done for them until they're adults and won't completely even then. As they experience seasons of life themselves, what you have sacrificed for them will slowly dawn on them. We must train our children because God expects us to and we only need to please God, not expect our kids' approval on each issue.

Secondly, expect your kids to need to question your values, the ones you've often fought for and been despised for by others. Your kids don't just grow up and adopt your beliefs as their own. They need time and freedom to question. Communication is a must. Talk things over with them. Allow space for questions without becoming defensive. Resist the temptation to feel threatened. Try to see things from their point of view. Hold strong to your values, but explain why you have the values you do and how you arrived at that conclusion. They'll come around to adopting them for themselves as you help them work through it.

It's kind of like getting saved. You can't just grow up in a Christian home and be a Christian. You have to deal with your sin and accept Jesus as your personal Lord. So it is with values. Your kids need room to think and reason and then adopt them and cling to them for themselves. Some will struggle more than others; be there to help and support and explain.

Be your child's best friend – not by dropping your standards, but by being there when *they* feel a need for you. Some of my best talks with my older kids have been between the hours of 11pm and 1am. When I see one lingering around after the others have headed off to bed, it's my cue that something's on their mind. I may be tired, I may need some quiet time myself, but remember, kids weren't given for our convenience.

Believe the best of your kids. Inspire them to greatness. Tell them how you expect God to use them to accomplish mighty acts. Pray with them. Pray for them. Take their burdens before God's holy throne in prayer. Help them to visualize God's plan for their life ("where there is no vision the people perish").

Ask God for vision for their lives. Encourage them to aspire to lofty things. Be positive. Don't always focus on the negatives. It's difficult to do, but don't let the negatives blind you to the positives. Tell them when you're pleased with them. Be interested in what interests them. Remember that every negative characteristic is a positive quality misused. God delights in taking our biggest weaknesses and making them our greatest strengths and areas of ministry to others.

Learn the power of enthusiasm! Anyone can learn. Your enthusiasm in their accomplishments or your vision for their life can be a powerful motivator. God created enthusiasm to help spur others to greatness. Watch how He uses it as you practice it in your relationship with your children and with others.

God is the mighty re-builder. If bitterness has sprung

up and caused rifts in your relationships, the first step is recognizing and acknowledging it, going back to your kids and confessing your sin. God will lead you in creativity to rebuild that relationship. It will take more work and more planning and more forgiving, as you are tempted to let that bitterness spring back up. Greater is He that is in us than he that is in the world.

When I stand before my Maker someday, I want to show him a perpetually godly generation, not a mess of broken lives scarred by bitterness.

You're the key – drop your load of bitterness at the Savior's feet and put your arm around your children. Come alongside them and be a Barnabas, encouraging them to give their all to the Savior! You'll be glad you did, for all eternity!

Chapter Twenty-One

Turning Loose

From babyhood to teens how time flies! Each stage has struggles, joys and rewards of its own. No, I don't believe teens have to rebel. They do need limits, some more than others, and they need our protection. There's no such thing as treating all kids equally, because they're all different. We must not let our standards down in the teen years just because it seems everyone else does. God is calling us to raise a godly standard.

In our house, freedoms are earned, not granted. Exercising responsibility earns freedoms. Freedoms wisely handled earn more freedoms. When freedom is abused, we withdraw freedoms until the teen has proved responsible again.

Freedom comes with being responsible, not age, and that level of responsibility will differ with each child. We had one child who thought that eighteen would be the magic age. It happened to be one who took longer to mature than most of the others. Eighteen was not the magic age!

Most of our kids were at least seventeen years old

before getting their drivers' license. When they did get their license, they were not allowed to just go places without permission. I want to know where my kids are. Just as we didn't allow them as kids to go running around the neighborhood, neither do we allow teens to go anywhere they choose.

Youth groups are not a part of our kids' experiences. Teens need to be maturing toward adulthood, not kept as kids, finding ways to entertain themselves. We allow our kids to be involved in adult functions at our church – choir, ushers, nursery, piano, singers, help with set up for functions, etc.

Our oldest daughter went on a missions trip with the senior saints to a mission in Virginia Beach. She helped paint the facility, serve lunch in the soup kitchen to the homeless, put on services, etc.

Three of our sons went on several missions trips, one to a Jamaican school for the deaf, one to Hungary and two to St. Thomas. They raked leaves on occasion with college kids for elderly folks. Life is about service, not play.

Our oldest son decided to go to college to obtain a degree in government. He paid for his own education by doing drywall on the side to put himself through school. He also got a job as opinion editor and later main editor for the college newspaper, which took up the vast majority of his time, but paid for half of his education and supplied him with a wonderful working knowledge of all the aspects of producing a paper. He also took CLEP tests and challenged courses, and completed his college career in three years instead of four. He graduated with a 3.8 GPA. By having to pay for his own education, he highly valued it and really desired to learn, and he got his money's worth.

My third son, on the other hand, apprenticed in drywall under Rick for several years and went out on his own at the age of nineteen and started his own drywall business. Yes, he's competition for Rick, but there's plenty of work in this area ...

He got married at 22, having established a very decent living before doing so.

Emily, who is nineteen, has started a house cleaning business and now has satisfied customers and her business is growing!

Carrie, seventeen, has a part-time business, a nanny job taking care of two kids two days a week.

Christa, sixteen, also does a large amount of babysitting, and also works for the Learning Parent, our home education ministry. She has valuable organizational skills and keeps things straight, as well as filling orders and packing products for conventions.

Laura loves to attend conventions with us and meet the people. She's a people person and has gotten to make many friends and see much of the country as well. She also has a ministry to elderly folks who delight to see her come to visit or get letters from her.

My children are very involved with people, just not in the ways most teens are, but in more adult roles. Rick and I frequently invite people into our home and try to encourage young parents just beginning their journey of parenting or home education.

Isn't that what it's all about anyway? Training our

children to become productive, caring adults who seek to serve the Lord and serve others? Press on, dare to do things different from the norm and your children will be different from the norm. They'll have a sense of purpose, direction and mission.

Chapter Twenty-Two

What Home Education Did For Our Family

This past summer I was working on a new presentation to give at conventions, "How We Began Homeschooling and Why I'm Glad We Did." I had set aside a whole Saturday to prepare what I wanted to say. I got my notebook and pen, got comfy in the recliner and prepared to organize my thoughts.

Just about that time, in came Tucker, my ten year old, running through the living room, dog barking and chasing at his heels. Matt turned on the music, looking for a song to sing in church. Kate, who was decorating a cake, was talking to Carrie and Emily, who were preparing something for the Sunday night supper bash. Tim and Kari stopped by to visit. Rick called to say he was dropping by to work on his taxes (which had to be done today) just in case he needed my help. Kelley and Kasey brought a story

134

they wanted me to read, and Gracie came in with her pet rooster, showing me how he crows on command. Laura began to scream because Tim was tickling her. Rick my husband came in the door, all excited about some new info he's just discovered, and by the way, do I have time today to talk to him as he does business planning? He's the kind of person who thinks by talking, and loves to run things by me. Tuck sits up next to me and says, "Maw, what do you figure?" which is his way of engaging you in conversation. "Can I have some lemonade?" Chris needs some ingredients for tomorrow, the laundry needed to be folded and some clothes need to ironed.

I was feeling pretty frustrated when God dropped an idea in my head. They're all here; ask them if and why they're glad they were home educated. I did, and was it ever exciting! This is what they told me, and they said it all better than I ever could.

 Rick has spent years in grassroots politics involvement; at age nineteen he became chairman of our county's Republican party. Ever since he was about twelve years old he's been helping conservative candidates get elected. Last November he won the seat of County Supervisor. Rick is a very intense person, throwing himself into whatever he does 100%. He has a call on his life from God to be a godly statesman. He desires to see godly principles returned to government as they once were.

Among his reasons for being glad he was home schooled were: "It taught me to care about real life issues and desire to make a difference in adult issues. I had the opportunity to be involved in the community while I was growing up. A plus was the opportunity to learn excellence for its own sake – learning to set a standard instead of fitting in to someone else's."

 Tim, our second son, is one of those people who can fix anything. We tried to give him the experience as a young boy of fixing many things that would break down around the house. He sees how things go together and he also is a master pianist, creating most of his own pieces. He is gifted with an ear for music and has a wonderful voice. Our Pastor commented on Tim as being unusual in that he gets along so well with people of all age groups.

Tim said, "I was taught a high work ethic. I'm not afraid to work hard. I learned to think for myself and value things besides just sports. I learned how to get an education – how to learn. I developed a strong appreciation of the simple things. We didn't have a lot of fancy entertainments, but we were hardly ever bored. We were forced to use our creativity."

 Nate was the first to get married, after having established his own business. Nate said, "I'm thankful I didn't spend the first eighteen years of my life in an unnatural situation – a slave of what people my own age thought and did. I never learned to care for pop culture, name brands, and fashions. I had the flexibility to explore interests, work opportunities, and special projects."

 Kate has recently begun traveling to conventions with us sometimes to speak. She has a passion for music and our country. She had this to say: "Watching my parents stand up for their beliefs and just being home schoolers back when they started and it wasn't accepted, made it easier to be different and stand alone for truth. You sort of got used to it. Home education has enabled me to have my own thoughts and think out of the box. It gave me time to write, create, start my own business, minister, teach art lessons to kids, and learn photography. It was kind of cool at work. Everyone had me stereotyped as a home schooled kid. Once you've proven yourself, though, you earn people's respect. It was interesting when our company did a huge lay-off, almost everyone but home schooled kids were laid off.

"I feel like my personal standards are higher than most kids' my age because of lack of constant peer pressure. I appreciated the opportunities to become involved in adult enterprises, such as speaking in a detention home for girls. I have friends of all ages. I can communicate with people without discomfort."

 Matt, 21, said "I appreciated not being stuck in school all day long, but still having the opportunity to learn more than if I'd been in school. I was taught the truth about American history, patriotism and creationism." Matt, who has a charming sense of humor, also said, "I graduated #1 in my class!"

He also said he benefited from lack of peer pressure, and not feeling a desire to be like everyone else. "There was no pressure to keep up with the Joneses. I don't feel inferior to drive a truck that's older than I am. I appreciated having individual attention as I needed it and an opportunity to progress at different rates in different subjects." This is one of my favorite things that he said, "I like the fact that I got to really know and appreciate my family instead of just meeting up with them in the evening."

 Emily, 19, has recently started a business and just purchased a 2001 GMC Jimmy that was wrecked. She had it fixed up and now drives a vehicle with fewer miles than any of ours. She plans to sell it in a year or two and do it again, so she can always drive something with low mileage. She said she was able to graduate early and go at her own pace. She was able to direct her own learning and instead of going through four years of college for piano, just take piano from a college professor and be instructed in what she wanted more practice in. "I had the opportunity to be involved in more during my school years and even start my own business and save money. I've learned how to set goals."

 Carrie, 17, just graduated this past June. Current events is her passion - seeing America turn back to God. Carrie says, "I learned real history instead of the watered-down version taught in public schools. I appreciated having the time to keep up with current events and know what's going on in our country. I'm able to listen to talk shows and be involved in the political process in a concrete way. I couldn't stand to be inside all day and told how to spend every minute." At this point in our family, it is Carrie's responsibility to prepare dinners, so she listens to talk shows as she works in the kitchen every afternoon.

Christa, 16, is indispensable to me in running the business and keeping our space organized and orders going out on time. Chris says, "I like the flexibility to do things." Chris has many babysitting jobs, and this past winter helped out a mom who had newborn, premature twins and a four and six year old also.

 Laura, 14, is great at convention time; she travels with us to many states. She loves meeting the people and is so skillful at running our table and explaining the materials. Laura says, "I like the special learning opportunities, like going to Appomattox and Williamsburg. I'm glad I can see the Ten Commandments, have prayer, and realize the importance of them. I appreciate the chance to have an interesting way of doing things instead of just learning through books. I'm glad I don't have to be on ritalin" (and she probably would have been!).

 Brittany Grace, often called Grace, now 13, is my animal lover. She spends many hours caring for her chickens, rabbit, cat, parakeets, tropical fish, and the family dog, as well as Rick's bloodhound he trains for the sheriff's department. She sells eggs to her married brothers, but mostly she keeps chickens for fun. She raised her rooster from a chick, and he crows on command, jumps for food, and comes when she calls him. She is recently enjoying helping her dad tame his horse. Animals love Gracie and vice versa.

When I asked her why she's glad she was home schooled, she answered, "You're not pushed and not slowed down. We're not forced to read books like 'Harry Potter'.

I'm glad to have time for my animals."

      Tucker, 10, is the guy with a math/science brain. He says, "I'm glad to be able to accomplish a whole lot more in a lot less time than if I went to school. I have time for lots of science experiments. We read things like 'From Log Cabin to White House', and have lots of time for history and practicing my aim on my BB gun and hunting."

      Kelley, age 7, is full of life and energy. She gets up in the morning wide awake and goes full speed until she crashes at bedtime. She speaks loudly and moves quickly and has just this past year learned to read, and loves to do so. She has a very giving heart. Kelley says, "It is much more interesting than what the neighbor girl said school is like. I'm glad I don't have homework and can go out to play when I finish."

      Kasey, 5, is our little patriot. Every night she prays that God will turn our country back to Him, and loves stories about George Washington and Nathan Hale and other patriots. She says, "I like getting treats for learning Bible verses. I like learning about George Washington. I like being home with you, Mommy."

They said it all! As for me, I wouldn't trade for anything the time and opportunity to get to really know my kids – each one individually – what makes them tick, and to be able to guide them in God's plan for their lives.

I delight in watching learning take place. There is a deep fulfillment in being there from the time your child began sounding out letters, then words, then finally takes off in reading. To watch their individual interests crop up and be able to provide books and materials and opportunities for each to explore those interests is great. To witness the process as each one learns from the others' interests is a treasure indeed.

I'm thankful for the opportunity home education affords to really invest in witnessing them make the right choices. It's such a blessing to hear of things your children have done, sometimes without you even knowing about it, to serve others. A widow in our church tells me of a time when shortly after her husband's death, Rick went to her house and installed motion-detector lights on her garage to surprise her. Another lady in our church told me of Josh, who when he actually had leukemia, stopped and pumped gas for her and her husband.

We've heard of others giving to needs within the church body from their own resources, so many instances that warm the heart of a parent. Our kids can accomplish so much more collectively than we can by ourselves. I love the responsibility and awesome privilege of training a newborn with all their potential from the Lord. I'm so grateful for the joy of being in a family that brings damage to Satan's kingdom. An added benefit is the wealth of information you learn that you never knew before. It's right and good and natural to learn with your kids. Don't ever feel you have to know it all to teach your kids.

Best of all, I love watching God's Word change lives (Heb. 4:12, "For the Word of God is quick, and powerful, and sharper than any two-edged sword, piercing even to the dividing asunder of soul and spirit, and of the joints and marrow, and is a discerner of the thoughts and intents of the heart").

Home education gave us the opportunity to build a close-knit family unit with a godly value system, looking for opportunities to serve our Savior with their lives! What could be any better?

☙ Chapter Twenty-Three

Leaving The Nest

The first one to leave was the hardest for me. My little family nest would never be the same again, but then I'm that kind of person who doesn't like change.

Nate was the first one to find the love of his life. Tina was the daughter of a missionary to Hungary, home on furlough for a year. We noticed that Nate would be just kind of standing around them, waiting to talk to Tina. Rick called him the Wooden Indian. We really liked Tina and her family, so we invited them to our house, and they reciprocated. Thus began lots of time spent with the Rices. The families got to know each other, and Nate and Tina got to know each other too.

When they returned to Hungary, Nate and Tina corresponded with each other, and Nate made a trip over there to visit Tina and see the mission field in Hungary. Nate and Tina were married in July of 2000.

Since then, Rick and Christina were married in July 2001, and Tim and Kari in April 2003.

We never let our kids 'date'. When they were interested in someone, we would have them over to the house often. In recent days we've designed Bible studies for a couple to do sometimes when they're together. We also have books and information we require prospective spouses to read. We allow short unsupervised dinner dates and things such as that, but we have to grant permission and know where they are and give a time to be back by.

Kate and Kevin have taken Kelley and Kasey out to one of the kids-eat-free-night restaurants. Our kids do a lot together, and couples sometimes go to functions at their siblings' houses, etc. They do need some time alone but under the right conditions and according to our guidelines.

We love our daughters-in-law. They have each made a wonderful addition to our family. We view our role as available counselor and helper, if needed, once our kids are married. We are available, but don't offer unsolicited advice. The new family needs time to bond and mold and grow and develop ties and traditions and convictions of its own. They are always welcome at our house and we want to help in any way we can, but otherwise, it's hands off. Our sons are the heads of their homes and need the freedom to set standards for their own family.

We've done our job. Now they're in God's hands, and God is powerful and doesn't need our help to lead His children.

I can honestly say I'm very pleased with the way our sons have established their families. In many ways our family has just been extended. We discuss holidays and try to work out a plan that suits everyone best. We all draw names at Christmastime so no one has too large a burden.

Our role is to encourage our sons and daughters to cleave to their spouse and support them, not to put pressure on them. That's my goal as a mother-in-law.

Chapter Twenty-Four

Me, A Grandma?

Our first grandchild is now about five weeks old, and a new one is due to be born in November. I'm entering another season. It's really kind of hard to comprehend that I'm actually a grandma!

I speak not with much experience on this issue, but with a huge dose of conviction. I've had so many grandparents comment that they can spoil their grandkids and send them home, but that's not my vision.

In Scripture, the only people mentioned time after time as trainers of children are parents and grandparents. I envision my role to be one of first, upholding the parent's values and wishes for their child. God ultimately holds parents responsible for the job of raising children, and they will answer to God for the job they did. Again, my role must be of support. Secondly, God does hold me accountable to be a positive spiritual influence in my grandchildrens' lives and that is what I purpose to be.

I envision reading them Bible stories and character building stories, teaching Scripture in creative ways when they come to visit, telling them stories of God's leading in history and my life and their parents' lives. If I were to watch my grandchildren when their parents weren't present, I would strive to follow the schedule and wishes of their parents and encourage the children to follow their wishes, thereby honoring God. I don't view my grandchildren as a toy to play with, but as a spiritual heritage to invest in.

The primary training must come from the parents, but grandparents should be a supplement and complement to parents whose lives are busy. I see a grandparent (although I'm not quite at this point yet) as one who has extra time to reinforce things the parents are teaching, one who has time to sit and read an extra story, or tell a story. I'm looking forward to being able to help supply my kids with quality books to teach their children with and hope to do some of the spiritual training projects with my grandchildren that I did with their parents.

I look forward to being able to give their parents a $20 bill and offer to watch their kids to give them a night out to enjoy being with each other, or watching the children sometimes to allow their mom to go shopping by herself. Cassidy has an aunt who is five years old, my youngest, Kasey. I envision them being good buddies. I had a sister who was five years older than me, and we had a great time playing dolls together for years. It's so healthy for kids to be around kids younger than them and learn to be a good example and develop a nurturing spirit.

So I look with anticipation to the years ahead. It's so nice to have a baby around the house again occasionally. I hope we'll be able to be a blessing to Tim and Kari and

Cassidy, and soon little Luke, also. Families are to help and support one another and cooperate on God's special mission for each one and for the family collectively. May God raise up the age-old foundations and may we be repairmen of the paths to dwell in (Isaiah 58:12). May we raise the banner high and show the world that God's way is best and His principles are good and right. God help us to pass on the torch to future generations!

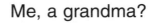

Chapter Twenty-Five

What Are We Working For, Anyway?

God has given me a vision. What I didn't realize all those years ago when we were following God's call on our lives and undergoing persecution was that God was planting like desires in hearts of moms and dads all across the nation! He was turning the hearts of fathers and mothers to their children. God was moving despite our ignorance, immaturity and fearfulness.

God called us to be pioneers in the home schooling movement, but I never realized that until many years later. We were following a burden on our hearts for our children, but God was moving mightily. Back then, even fellow Christians thought we were crazy for not putting our kids in school. Although we didn't try to convince others that they should do it (unless of course they felt God was leading them to), I think it was a threat to many. If we were right, maybe they ought to consider it. It was easier to call us lunatics.

School materials were difficult to obtain. Suppliers didn't want to sell to parents. Socialization was a huge issue! We did what we felt compelled to do and hoped to be right, but we had no proof.

Today, the proof is there. Dr. Brian Ray has done lots of testing and surveying, and has found that home educated kids do considerably better than their publicly educated counterparts. They tend to be leaders, not followers. Academically, we did our best and prayed that it was enough. Now we know home educated kids are winning national spelling bees and geography bees. Colleges are pursuing home educated kids because they have proven to be self-motivated learners.

One president of a well-known Christian college near us, who used to be opposed to home education, recently held a small home education convention at his school and told parents that of all three "classes" of kids entering his school, home educated ones far surpass the others. Christian and private schools rank next best, with public schools trailing in the rear.

Businesses prefer home educated kids. Chick FIL-A hires home educated kids above others, as they've proven to be diligent, competent workers.

Back in 1982, we had no inkling that we were on the edge of a movement that would sweep across the country. David Barton, in "Reformation vs. Revival," says that reformation always brings about lasting changes in the society. People often don't realize while in the midst of it, but later look back and say, "Oh, so that's what God was doing!"

Rick and I travel across the country and I am finally seeing what God has been and is now doing through your children! I'm excited now more than ever at what your children and mine are going to accomplish for God.

Rick recently had a thirty-five year old employee who didn't know who our first president was. Some high school grads can't find the USA on the map of the world. Millions of kids are being drugged on ritalin or being labeled learning disabled unnecessarily.

Our godly heritage as a nation has been stolen from us, but it excites me that God is raising up people like David Barton and others to research and rediscover our godly heritage.

Our republic was founded on biblical principles. We have the holy privilege of recovering this information and teaching our children the truth. Christians used to be the head, not the tail. Civil leaders would ask counsel of ministers and pastors. Pastors would preach sermons on election day, current events and happenings, by going to scripture to see what it had to say about all these things.

Mike Farris, last fall at a leadership convention for home school leaders, said he believed we are the Moses generation. We had to take the flock to leave Egypt. Our children are the Joshua generation who will take the land. I believe we'll see our children's generation lead this country back to godly principles. Mike pointed out that Joshua didn't get the land all at once. He had to fight many battles one by one, little by little, town by town.

We have many battles ahead, but I believe our children will shine as lights in the midst of a dark world, that we will once again see Christians be the salt and light to our nation and recover surrendered ground in all walks of life.

You moms and dads – you are my heroes! What you're going to do is the right thing to do. God is moving. You and your children were born into this spot in history for a reason, and God is again raising a standard in our land! Press on! Follow that prompting in your heart to give your best to your children – for the Lord's sake!

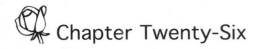 Chapter Twenty-Six

From My Heart To Yours

As a piece of closing advice from a mom of fourteen, please:

Take time to rock your baby. Rock and sing and whisper of how special he is to God – of his mission to live for God and lead others to the Savior by the life he lives. Take time to play in the sandbox with him, as he grows a little older. When you build those castles in the sand, you're really building for eternity.

Take time to delight in him as God delights in us. Let him know you love him by the time you spend with him. Take time to listen to him when he feels a need to talk to you. Don't wait for a convenient time. Children weren't given for our convenience. We need to say no to things of lesser eternal value, and listen to him.

Take time to teach him right from wrong. Tell him when he learns to obey mommy and daddy that he is really obeying God. Help him learn while he's little so he won't have to learn the hard way when he's older.

Take time to hold him. The day will come sooner than you wish when he'll be too big to hold on your lap, and you'll wish he could be little again, even for just one day. Take time to be excited about all the little things that excite him. When all is said and done, it seems that what is really important in life and what sticks in your memory and lasts for eternity is all those little things.

Take time to make all the memories today you want your child to have tomorrow.

Take time to live with eternity in your hearts. Ask God to make clear those opportunities He wants you to take and give you the grace to take up your cross daily and follow Him.

Take the time when he grows older to be his friend. Take time to be the kind of parent that points that little life to Jesus. Invest your time in teaching him God's Word. Make it a priority.

Take time to give your child the security of knowing he has your heart, and in so doing, making it easier for him to freely give his heart back to his Creator and Heavenly Father. That is, after all, our mission.

Live, making plans for tomorrow, but also as if this were your last day on earth.

God bless each one of you as you invest your lives in the most precious things on earth – the lives of your little ones!

APPENDICES

Appendix 1
'The Teaching Home' article, 10/98

Article from "The Teaching Home" magazine, Oct. 1, 1998

"Young Mom Has 14 Gifts"

I've always thought of myself as a young mom. Rickey, our oldest, was born on my twentieth birthday. Today I sent our 15-year-old son Matthew outside to put the new license plates on our 15-passenger van. They read, 14 GIFTS. Kasey Lynne, our 14th gift (Ps. 127:3), was born two days ago. That makes eight girls and six boys. One week ago Rick and I celebrated our birthdays. Rick turned 24. Tucker, our 5-year-old, asked, "Mom, how old will you be when I turn 24?"

I quickly did the addition in my head, but was I stunned! Like I said, I've always thought of myself as a young mom. I am — to our oldest children. Tuck pursued the question with a few other inquiries: "How old will you be when I'm __ ?" I finally had to put a stop to it. It unnerves me to think of it. I still feel like a young mom!

Last night Kasey slept so well. I should have, too, but I lay awake holding Kasey, watching her, listening to her breathing and all the little sounds she made — just praising God for the privilege of raising another child to serve Him. What a joy to watch His plan unfold for each one.

Nighttime feedings have never been a bother to me. I welcome them. The house is quiet — yes, quiet! It's a time for me to reflect, to commune with the Lord, to enjoy my baby without any interruptions. Last night I just basked in the miracle of birth, the awesome potential of this tiny one sent from God for me to direct toward Him. I was overflowing with gratitude that once again God has allowed me the privilege to be a new mom.

I may not be a young mom anymore, but looking back, I would never trade the way I've spent my life for anything in the world — not a career, not fame, not wealth. I'm one of the richest people in the world. I have a wonderful husband and 14 precious, thoroughly unique gifts from God. I've watched as each one grows, walks, talks, learns to read, and blossoms in God-given areas of interest.

I've directed my energies in teaching our children God's Word and watched as God molds each into the person He wants them to be. I've even watched as God took our 17-year-old home to heaven after he suffered with leukemia for seven months. Death and life are in God's control.

I'm so thankful for each of my 14 gifts. Life wouldn't have been complete without the dimension each has added to our lives. With each one I've learned a little bit more about what our God is like.

As I pour my life into the lives God has entrusted to me, He stands above me as He did for the widow of Shunem and fills me to overflowing from His never-empty vessel of grace. Yes, children truly are a gift of the Lord. And I still am a young mom — at heart, anyway!

Marilyn Boyer, Virginia

Appendix 2
Character Qualities for a Mom

Flexibility – not being too busy to stop folding laundry to go see the queen ant that Tuck just dug up

Generosity – is sharing the last piece of cake you'd been saving to enjoy in a quiet moment because Laura just joined you on the swing and this is an opportunity to show her she is pretty special to you

Gentleness – is putting your arm around your son and reaffirming your love for him when he just made a bad decision you advised him against and he's sorry for it

Gratefulness – is thanking God for the privilege of parenthood and how it is a picture of our relationship with our Heavenly Father, not a hindrance to our serving Him

Humility – is admitting you blew it when you lose your cool at first look at the lemonade all over the kitchen floor

Initiative – is acting on those "ideas" that just seem to pop into your head (they are really promptings from God) like, "Kelley REALLY needs more of your attention!!"

Joyfulness – is realizing God has given me everything I need today to live in His victory and that He turns our greatest sorrows into our deepest joys

Decisiveness – is choosing to make that tough decision to limit your child's association with unprofitable friends because you know it's the right thing to do

Creativity – is asking God to show us ways to make mundane tasks enjoyable. (Tuck is an expert at this)

Alertness – is sending out those spiritual sensors that only MOM can to spot potential dangers in my kids' lives

and taking steps to remove them

Boldness – is facing confrontations with assurance that God will bless the outcome if I'm standing in His truth

Dependability – is always being there to listen and lift them up and help point them to Jesus

Meekness – is yielding our rights to God so we don't get angry when our kids don't do just what we expect of them

Obedience – is to purpose to appropriate God's grace to do what we know is right even when we just don't feel like it

Orderliness – is doing our best to find a place for everything thereby making it easier for our children to be orderly

Patience – is welcoming trials by turning them into projects from God to conform us to be like Jesus

Persuasiveness – is sharing with our kids how God's ways are working in our lives so they'll want to follow Him

Resourcefulness – is turning that juice can Kelley decorated into a pencil holder

Sensitivity – is comforting instead of belittling or laughing at your child when they make a silly mistake

Forgiveness – is picturing how Jesus died on the cross for my sins so that God's love can flow through me to heal my children's hurts

Deference – is giving up spending the day scrapbooking just for fun as you'd planned, to help Rick pass out literature because he's responsible to get the job done and needs help

Appendix 3
Rick Jr.'s word from 'Fun Projects"

A quick note of corroboration, just to show that the ones most affected by these projects still remember them and they really do work. The one I remember best is probably the 'Ifs'. Mom used to do those with us, it seemed, most every day. Almost every time I would stop to consider what I was about to do I would think, "If this happened, what would you do?" It was more often than not the stop sign I needed.

The Character Sketch quilts were probably Mom's best investment of time out of all the projects. I abandoned mine only a couple of years ago, because the poor thing was 12 or 15 years old and sadly threadbare. I still have it in the closet, of course, and still occasionally stop and mentally thank Mom for her investment of time and character for me.

For you hassled moms too, I can't say enough about 'Training Sessions' at the supermarket. Of course in our case there was always some doubt as to whether we were more out of the way in a straight line or in a tight group. I never really got into the habit of reaching for things from the shelves or repeating, "Mom, let's get this, Mom, let's get that." With Dad acting as traffic policeman, Mom was able to get her shopping done with much less trouble, until eventually it was just habit and Dad didn't have to be there to protect the store's property.

I could say more about most of these ideas, but I will just say one more thing: Thanks, Mom and Dad.

Appendix 4
Bible ABC's

A Abraham . . . . .Gen. 15:6
   Adam . . . . .I Cor. 15:22
B Boy . . . . .John 4
   Barnabas Heb.10:25
C Caleb . . . . .Num. 14:24
D David . . . . .I Sam. 17:37
   Daniel . . . . .Dan. 6:22
   Deborah . . . . .Judges 4:14
E Eve . . . . .Gen. 3:20
   Elijah Matt.6:26
F Fishers of Men . . .Matt.4:19
   Farmer Matt.13:24
   Father . . . . .Luke 15:32
G Gideon . . . . .Judges 7:7
   Good Samaritan . . .Luke 10:33
H Hezekiah . . . . . . .II Kings 18:5
   Hannah . . . . .I Sam. 1:27-28
I Isaiah . . . . .Gen. 21:2-3
J Jesus . . . . .Luke 2:52
   Joseph . . . . .Gen. 45:5,7
   Joash . . . . .II Chr. 24:1-2
   Josiah . . . . .II Kings 22:2
   Joshua . . . . .Josh. 24:15
K King David . . . . . .II Sam. 9:7
   King Solomon . . . .I Kings 3:9-14
L Lazarus . . . . .John 11:25-26, 43
M Matthew Matt.9:9

Moses . . . . .Heb. 24-25

Mary . . . . .Luke 2:7

N Nicodemus . . . . .John 3:16

  Noah . . . . .Gen. 9:1

O Obadiah . . . . . . .I Kings 18:3

  Obed-edom . . . . .II Sam. 6:12

P Paul . . . . .Acts 16:25, 30-31

Q Queen Esther . . .Est. 4:14

R Ruth . . . . .Ruth 2:12

S Samuel . . . . . . .I Sam.3:10

  Simeon . . . . . . .Luke 2:27-29

  Shunamite woman .II Kings 4:36-37

T Timothy . . . . . . .II Tim. 3:15

U Unique . . . .(picture of your child) Ps. 139:14-15

V Virtuous woman . .Prov. 31:10

W Widow . . . . .Luke 21:3-4

X Xerxes . . . . .Est. 8:1

Y Young children . . .Mark 10:14

Z Zachaeus . . . . . .Luke 19:8-9

  ZachariusLuke 1:6,13

*Pictures for all these people can be found in the following coloring books (available from www.thelearningparent.com):
Reproducible Coloring Book
Bible Story Time
Thru the Bible Coloring Pages

Appendix 5
Recommended Resources

All these resources are available through our catalog or at
www.thelearningparent.com.

A Full Quiver Rick and Jan Hess, 1989

Child's Book of Character Building vol. 1 and 2
available from the Learning Parent

Five Love Languages of Children Gary Smalley and
Ross Campbell, 1997

Fun Projects for Hands-On Character Building Rick
and Marilyn Boyer, 1996

God's Little Wonders Sandra Kuck, Harvest House
Publishers 2002

Growing Up A Country Boy Donald Zolan, Harvest
House Publishers 2004

Jesus Plaque print available from the Learning Parent

Lives of the Signers B.J. Lossing, reprinted by
Wallbuilders 2002

Nativity Cookie Cutters available from the Learning Parent

Take Your Hat Off When the Flag Goes By available
from the Learning Parent

The Name Book Dorothy Astoria, Bethany House
Publishers 1987

Uncle Rick Reads the Proverbs Rick and Marilyn
Boyer, available from the Learning Parent

What Little Boys Are Made Of Sandra Kuck, Harvest
House Publishers 2000

What Little Girls Are Made Of Sandra Kuck, Harvest
House Publishers, 2001

Appendix 6
Scripture Verses on Conception

Babies are not simply a "product of conception" – God controls conception

Eve – "I have gotten a manchild with the help of the Lord" <u>Gen. 4:1</u>

Hagar – Angel of the Lord said to her, "I will greatly multiply your descendants that they shall be too many to count." <u>Gen. 16:10</u>

Abraham – God promises him "I will multiply you exceedingly."

Abimelech – "And Abraham prayed to God and God healed Abimelech and his wife and his maids, so that they bore children. For the Lord had closed fast all the wombs of the household of Abimelech because of Sarah, Abraham's wife." <u>Gen. 21:1-2</u>

Sarah – "The Lord took note of Sarah as He had said and the Lord did for Sarah as He had promised. So Sarah conceived and bore a son to Abraham in his old age, at the appointed time of which God had spoken to him." <u>Gen. 21:1-2</u>

Rachael and Leah – <u>Gen. 29:31 – Gen. 30:24</u>

"He opened her womb." <u>Gen. 29:31</u>

"He has therefore given me this son also." <u>Gen. 29:33</u>

"Am I in the place of God, who has withheld children from you?" <u>Gen. 30:2</u>

"God has vindicated me...and has given me a son." <u>Gen. 30:6</u>

"And God gave heed to Leah and she conceived." <u>Gen. 30:17</u>

"And God gave heed to her and opened her womb." <u>Gen. 30:22</u>

Moses – God conceives and brings forth – "Was it I who conceived all these people? Was it I who brought them forth?" <u>Num. 11:12</u>

Ruth – "And the Lord enabled her to conceive, and she gave birth to a son." <u>Ruth 4:13</u>

Samuel – The Lord closed and the Lord opened – "Her rival however, would provoke her bitterly to irritate her, because the Lord had closed her womb." <u>I Sam. 1:6</u>

"And Elkanah had relations with Hannah his wife, and the Lord remembered her. And it came about in due time, after Hannah had conceived, that she gave birth to a son." <u>I Sam. 1:19</u>

"And the Lord visited Hannah; and she conceived and gave birth to three sons and two daughters." <u>I Sam. 2:20-21</u>

David – God planned you – <u>Psalm 139: 13-16</u>

Ezekiel – God causes population growth – "I made you numerous [literally a myriad] like plants of the field." <u>Ez. 16:7</u>

Psalm 100 – "It is He who has made us, and not we ourselves."

Elizabeth – "…This is the way the Lord has dealt with me in the days when He looked with favor upon me, to take away my disgrace among men." <u>Luke 1:24-25</u>

Hebrews – "I will surely bless you, and I will surely multiply you." <u>Heb. 6:14</u>

"By faith even Sarah herself received ability to conceive, even beyond the proper time of life, since she considered Him faithful who had promised." <u>Heb. 11:11</u>

Jesus – Conception without fertilization

<u>Psalm 37:25</u> – How do I feed them?
<u>Psalm 127</u> – Children are a gift, reward
<u>Psalm 128</u> – Fruitful wife is a blessing

The Myth of Overpopulation*

The world is comparatively empty. There are 52.5 million square miles of land are in the world, not including Antarctica.

If all the people in the world were brought together into one place, they could stand, without touching anyone else, in less than 200 square miles...

If all the people in the world came together in one place and stood shoulder to shoulder, they would all fit within one-half of the city limits of Jacksonville, Florida with plenty of room to spare!

The world population is four and a half billion people. By allowing an average of 2.6 square feet for each person from babies to adults, every person in the world could stand shoulder to shoulder in just one-half of the city.

A further fallacy in the population explosion myth is the assumption that the greater the population, the lower the standard of living. This is not true. Japan has a population density of 798 people per square mile, yet they have a higher per capita gross national product ($,450) than India, which has 511 people per square mile ($140).

Projections of running out of energy or food sources are totally misleading. God gave to man the command and ability to fill up the world with people and to subdue the earth for their own needs.

India does not have a hunger problem because of lack of food. It has a hunger problem because of religious beliefs which are contrary to the Word of God. The Hindu religion teaches that people who die are reincarnated in the form of animals; thus it is against their laws and religion to kill rats, mice, cows, or other animals.

Every cow eats enough food to feed seven people, and there are two hundred million "sacred cows" in India. If the people of India would just stop feeding these cows, they would have enough food to feed one billion, four hundred million people. That is more than one-fourth of the entire world's population!

God promises adequate provision for those who serve Him and obey His laws. On the other hand, He warns that those who reject His Word will experience destructive hunger and famine.

*Excerpts from <u>How to Understand Humanism,</u> an Institute in Basic Life Principles Publication.